THE
GUADALCANAL
AIR WAR

THE GUADALCANAL AIR WAR

Col. Jefferson DeBlanc's Story

JEFFERSON J. DEBLANC

PELICAN PUBLISHING COMPANY

GRETNA 2008

To my wife, Louise Berard DeBlanc, and our
five children, who continually inspire me

The word "Pelican" and the depiction of a pelican
are trademarks of Pelican Publishing Company, Inc.,
and are registered in the U.S. Patent and Trademark Office.

Library of Congress Cataloging-in-Publication Data

DeBlanc, Jefferson J., 1921-2007.
  The Guadalcanal air war : Col. Jefferson DeBlanc's story / by Jefferson J. DeBlanc.
     p. cm.
  Includes bibliographical references.
  ISBN 978-1-58980-587-3 (hbk. : alk. paper) 1. DeBlanc, Jefferson J., 1921-2007. 2. Guadalcanal, Battle of, Solomon Islands, 1942-1943–Personal narratives, American. 3. World War, 1939-1945–Aerial operations, American. 4. World War, 1939-1945–Personal narratives, American. 5. Air pilots, Military–United States–Biography. I. Title.
  D767.98.D43 2008
  940.54'265933–dc22

                                               2008006195

Printed in the United States of America

Published by Pelican Publishing Company, Inc.
1000 Burmaster Street, Gretna, Louisiana 70053

Contents

**PART THREE FULL CIRCLE FOR A
                   CACTUS AIR FORCE FIGHTER PILOT**

PART ONE

THE BAND BEGINS TO PLAY

O it's Tommy this, an' Tommy that, an' "Tommy go away";
But it's "Thank you, Mister Atkins," when the band begins to play. . . .
                                                    Rudyard Kipling

Chapter 1

A Boyhood Presage

By the early 1900s,* my father was a brakeman on the Southern Pacific Railroad. He married Noelie Zoe Barras on November 4, 1912. To protect his job, my family moved frequently to various Louisiana towns. So it was that I was born in Lockport on February 15, 1921, the youngest of five children. Shortly thereafter, my family moved to Port Barre and remained there until the Great Depression.

Although I played cowboys and Indians with my friends, I always wore a Captain Eddie Rickenbacker flying suit, complete with Sam Browne belt and goggles! I was truly hooked on flying.

Sometime during the 1920s, a two-seater biplane, flying the U.S. mail or barnstorming, made a forced landing in a cow pasture about one mile from my home in Port Barre, Louisiana. I remember running all the way to the site with my childhood companions, Ellis Resweber, Sammy Bryant, and Alida "Sis" Bryant. As a "reward" for arriving first, the pilot lifted me up for a quick look into the cockpit. I was transfixed by the instrument panel with its gauges, dials, switches, all precision-made and, to me, incomprehensible, but with an elusive, underlying pattern.

*At this time, spectrum analysis, electromagnetism, the atomic theory in chemistry, the molecular composition of gas, and the measurement of the velocity of light were widely discussed, though little understood.

As it turned out, this was truly a defining moment in my life! This makeshift, emergency landing strip in a cow pasture near my boyhood home presaged another airstrip far away from home in miles and in years on the battle-scarred island of Guadalcanal, in a cow pasture there known as Fighter One.

The Atchafalaya River cuts through the south-central Louisiana swamps as it makes its way to the Gulf of Mexico. Levees were constructed on its banks to protect the countryside from flooding when the high water came. In the spring of 1927, the Atchafalaya River levee collapsed at Melville, a town some fifteen miles northeast of Port Barre as the crow flies, flooding much of the south-central Louisiana countryside with eight to twelve feet of water.

Traveling in my father's Model T Ford, we visited Melville the week before to get a glimpse of the action we had heard about but doubted. Communications left a lot to be desired in those days. All we had in our home were crystal radios and regenerative sets. Superheterodyne radios—which mix the frequency of the received radio signal with another locally generated signal and convert them to an intermediate frequency to assist amplification and filter undesirable signals—were in the future. The rising water was awesome and the sight of men working in twelve-hour shifts, sandbagging the levee at various weak spots, was frightening.

The roads were muddy and full of potholes. A trip from Port Barre to Melville, requiring today little more than half an hour, took hours then. The return trip on the winding swamp road, enhanced every now and then by a chance encounter with an alligator, was completed in record time with the Model T huffing and puffing. The stately automobile retained its dignity without even a flower out of place in the vases flanking both doors inside—a luxury item in the 1926 vintage Ford. These vases separated the deluxe model from the standard one and were a status symbol.

We were among the residents* of Port Barre who fled before the levee broke, going to St. Martinville, a town some fifty miles to the south. But when the water began to reach the three-foot level there, we departed for Cade, a settlement located on a bluff five miles away. We were now free to watch the water rise over the countryside. We were lucky to have an entire second-floor screened porch as our home away from home until the waters receded.

Biplanes flew over the area to survey the damage and to find people stranded by the flooding. I was fascinated by the maneuvers of these aircraft as I viewed them from the rooftop of our quarters. I did not know that the planes I saw were taking aerial photos of the disaster below. From these flights, a plan would evolve to place two great levees, the east and the west guide levees, from Melville to the Gulf of Mexico. This project would funnel the spring waters from the north.

There was a price to be paid for this little gem. What nature had developed in a thousand years, man destroyed in ten.

---

*There were six of us—Frank and Noelie (my parents), Marie, Frank, Marguerite, and me. My father had enough seniority to guarantee his railroad job. He worked the run from New Iberia to Mamou. We moved to St. Martinville because of the flood and the depression. Learning to drive became necessary for me since my father depended on some member of the family to drive him the nine miles from St. Martinville to the depot in New Iberia. (My dad died on December 30, 1961, and my mother on January 25, 1977. One of my sisters, Mathilde, born after Marie and before Frank, had died of diphtheria when she was very young. Marie died on April 21, 1995, and Frank on January 25, 1999. [May 2001 note])

Many beautiful old live oaks, large cypresses, and various other kinds of hardwoods and softwoods would soon disappear in the Atchafalaya Basin because of the rising land elevation caused by siltation.

Yet the project helped many of us orient ourselves in the swamp. The southward flow of water at high speed left the north side of tree trunks bare and their south sides with hanging streaks of debris. Only a city novice would get lost in the Basin. All one had to do was not panic if lost, but simply set a course east or west by moving ninety degrees across the tree lines until clear of the swamps.

There is a little saying among the Acadians, who like to play solitaire, that a hunter in the swamps should bring along a deck of cards. In case he got lost, the hunter would simply sit down, start playing solitaire, and within thirty seconds someone would surely come along to watch the game and perhaps say, "Put the red 'ten' on the black 'jack'!"

Chapter 2

The Great Depression

The Thirties entered with a bang. The Great Depression was in full swing. President Franklin Delano Roosevelt had introduced his National Recovery Act, symbolized by a decal of an eagle grasping arrows in its talons, a patriotic emblem for almost every home in America. W.P.A.* jobs were in abundance. The Civilian Conservation Corps was created to get people back to work and to heal the wounds of the Civil War through a demographic reshuffling. In plain language, Southern boys went north and Northern boys came south. The Evangeline State Park in St. Martinville was enhanced by the labor of New York and New Jersey men in the C.C.C., many of whom married Southern belles and settled down in Louisiana.

Huey Long, the "Kingfish," had passed on into history, having made his contributions of free textbooks, paved highways, hospitals, and "Every Man a King" in Louisiana. This was also the time of the Lindbergh tragedy, details of which filtered down even to Louisiana. In a few years, fortune would place Lindbergh and me face to face!

By 1931, tent movies were all over the South. Movie houses were unheard of, except in big cities. Traveling tent shows were something to see. After school, we would watch the crew pitch

*Work Projects Administration.

the huge tent and assemble wooden chairs for the evening 35mm movie. Rin Tin Tin movies or Westerns were usually advertised on posters outside the tent area. I waited eagerly for the aviation movies which depicted the World War.

The price of admission was five cents for children and ten cents for adults, but there was a gimmick the movie owners pulled to get extra money. Between reel changes during a seven-reel movie, the lights would come on and beautiful Indian blankets would be displayed. Boxed candy was sold and the owner would mention something about a special coin that could be found in one of the candy boxes, giving the lucky winner the blanket of his choice. You guessed it! What the winner saw and what he received were two very different blankets. But it worked and many of the "rich" moviegoers were fleeced.

The movies were great for a wide-eyed youngster growing up in the Acadian country. I managed to talk the projectionist out of a few feet of aircraft 35mm leader and other discarded pieces of film. Thirty-five-millimeter home projectors were a novelty in those days and we had one. I drove the rest of the family nuts with my spliced film of Rin Tin Tin, horse operas, and flying aces.

Most of my older friends joined the C.C.C. and attended summer camp. We were awed and held in suspense at the tales of rifle firing and military training they received. These were not the days of television and other such attractions. The status symbol of the youth of 1932 was a belt buckle on which was stamped in bas-relief "C.M.T.C." (Civilian Military Training Corps) and an American eagle. One was a "peasant" (Huey Long's *Every Man a King!*) without such a buckle. This vicarious exposure to military life and survival training would prove an asset to me during World War II.

My interest in flying was enhanced by the comic books of the

Thirties, G-8 and his Flying Aces, for example. By the age of thirteen, I knew most of the German, British, French, and American aces of the Great War and the tactics they used. My father spoke so often about Alcibiades De Blanc and his exploits in the Civil War that I dreaded hearing about him. So intense was my desire for flying that I could less identify with the ground troops.

But I also remembered ground-war stories from my cousin Louis Bertrand ('T Goose), who fought in France during World War I. Tragically, he would be killed in 1943 when the Merchant Marine ship that he was aboard was torpedoed in the Gulf of Mexico by a German U-Boat.*

By the time I entered high school in St. Martinville, I was reading accounts of the Spanish Civil War. Life magazine covered the war pretty well, but not enough to reflect the concept of a proving ground for fighter aircraft. This appeared to be so for Germany, Italy, and Russia, nations exploiting the air action as a research field for future fighter planes.

By 1938, the tension in Europe began to flare. Air training movies, such as *The Hell Divers* featuring Robert Taylor, appeared in the movie houses and tents throughout the United States. I remember *The Fighting 69th* with James Cagney, a movie intended to arouse patriotism.

During this time, I began to secretly admire a St. Martinville beauty, Louise Berard, whom I was to marry after the war. During high-school days, we both played forward position on our respective basketball teams. Her team went to State in 1936 and won. Our boys' team did not get to State, but we had excellent games.

*Years later, I was best man at his son's marriage. Joseph "Joe Joe" Bertrand is now an attorney in New Orleans.

Chapter 3

Bridging the Gap in Flight Training

The Second World War began on September 1, 1939, when Germany invaded Poland. Britain, France, Australia, and New Zealand declared war on Germany on September 3. Subsequently, Germany successfully invaded the Low Countries and France. Italy then joined in the war, occupying part of North Africa. In an about-face, Hitler turned on the Soviet Union.

Throughout this time, Japan depended upon the United States for scrap iron, oil, cotton, and metals. What we sold them would soon be shot back at us in the modified, lethal form of bullets and bombs!

As the action heated up in Europe in 1939, the United States Congress, realizing the shortage of pilots in our country, passed the Civilian Pilot Training Act, enabling our colleges to offer a pilot training program as part of their curricula. This was an attempt to bridge the gap in aviation that existed in all branches of the service, a lag that almost proved detrimental to the country.

During its first three years, the C.P.T. trained more than 100,000 young college men and women civilians, a reserve on which the armed forces drew heavily for pilot material. Many leading aces, including Captain Joe Foss of the Marine Corps and Captain Richard Bong (now deceased) of the Army Air Corps, started with the C.P.T.

Needless to say, I enrolled in one of the first C.P.T. classes at Southwestern Louisiana Institute,* Lafayette, Louisiana. In a class of twenty-one students, I was one of two who soloed during the prescribed time. On February 8, 1940, I was issued license number 48857-1940 by the Civil Aeronautics Authority. The planes we flew were 50-horsepower Piper cubs.

The U.S. Navy had less than 6,300 pilots at the time of Pearl Harbor. Before wartime expansion, pilot training consisted of a modest course designed to weed out the obviously unfit, followed by six months of flight training and such amounts of further training with the fleet as circumstances allowed. This program was expanded until February 1942, when a full wartime course was implemented, requiring twenty months to complete. I trained under this first draft, a rush job to get bodies to the front as quickly as possible, to act as a buffer until "properly trained" pilots could be phased into aviation. The pilots in the service before World War II were an "elite" group and resented the influx of many "college boys" joining the ranks. Correspondedly, the washout factor was high among aviation cadets all through 1941.

It is noteworthy to compare our flight time with these future pilots. We left for combat with barely 250 hours of flight training and hardly any training in firing guns and in dogfighting tactics. These other men were given a minimum of 500 hours of flight instructions plus the following features. The aviation cadets—all volunteers and all carefully screened and selected to secure none but the best, mentally and physically—were first given preliminary academic work at flight preparatory schools established at twenty colleges throughout the country. This was

*Today, the University of Louisiana at Lafayette (ULL).

followed by preliminary ground schools and very elementary flight training at ninety-two war training service schools at these twenty colleges and at military aviation fields around the nation, all under the supervision of the Civil Aeronautics Authority. The trainees were given a strenuous course in physical training, including boxing, wrestling, swimming, football, hand-to-hand combat, labor engineering, and military track, the latter being on obstacle courses which became well known features on many college campuses. Survival techniques were also taught. Courses were designed to bring future fliers to the peak of physical condition and to give them the alertness and quick reflexes so necessary for combat fighting, together with the ruggedness and endurance essential for survival if forced down on land or sea beyond our lines.

Those who passed this training were then sent to one of five preflight schools to receive training up to and including soloing. Long Beach, Kansas City, New Orleans, Great Lakes, and Floyd Bennett Field* were the Navy's five elimination schools.

After this training, they were sent to one of three flight schools (Pensacola, Corpus Christi, and Jacksonville) for fourteen weeks of ground school and flying. As the program began to catch up with the wartime demands for pilots and as facilities expanded, even more training could be given to these men already considered the best trained aviators in the world. We called them "supermen" and had to agree that they were better trained than we.

---

*Floyd Bennett Field is now La Guardia Airport, New York.

Chapter 4

A Dunk in Lake Pontchartrain

The Navy required in 1939 four years of college for the aviation program because of the mathematics and navigational problems aboard aircraft carriers. My brother, Frank, had his degrees in civil and electrical engineering by this time. With the draft breathing down his neck, he made preparations to obtain a commission with Army engineers. He discussed this with me.

I was "brainwashed" on aviation and took Frank up for a flight in a Piper cub, explaining to him how one could easily be killed in the engineering corps, earmarked as it was for front line activities. Flying over the enemy, on the other hand, was parttime business and safer. Combat would be almost on one's own terms instead of on a twenty-four-hour basis. He bought my arguments and after we landed, he headed for the Navy recruiting station.

Entering the aviation cadet flying program, he was sent to Pensacola, Florida, and later to Jacksonville for flight training. He breezed through the program, emerging as an Ensign.* He became a pilot of a PBY-5, a twin-engined heavy float plane

*There are many types of pilots: fighter pilots, bomber pilots, commercial pilots, torpedo bomber pilots. The ones who fly these different types of planes are not of the same "breed." Frank was born to be an instrument pilot. As we shall see, he did such an outstanding job on instruments that the Navy would pull him from combat to fly the Gulf of Mexico during hurricane season.

used by the Navy for reconnaissance, antisubmarine patrol, and convoy escort.

I naturally wanted to follow in his footsteps. But I wanted fighters. I was working toward my degree when the requirements were dropped to three years of college to expedite more aviators for the fleet. At nineteen years of age with the draft looking down my throat, I enlisted. *Ab initio,* my desire for military flying was enhanced by an added bonus of $500 per year for every year served (up to four years), payable upon separation, under clause "J" of the contract. The terms of the contract were four years from the date of commitment, provided you signed up before a shooting war occurred. For a young man working his way through college, this was of intrinsic value to me, sort of having my cake and eating it too. I passed the tests, physical and mental, and became on July 29, 1941, a Seaman Second Class and a potential Naval aviation cadet, stationed in New Orleans.

It was a culture shock for me when I reported for training at the New Orleans E-base, an elimination flight training base. After having led a quiet, sheltered life, I found myself "breaking bread" with Yankees of all types, sons of college professors, doctors, teachers, and bankers. These Ivy League college men quickly appeared to take over. Most of them were familiar with Navy protocol and terminology, which was a little difficult for us Southern boys to swallow. However, we survived this phase of Naval training and got down to the common denominator— flying. All else was a game to be played and tolerated.

The trainer we flew was the N3N, an all-fabric, open cockpit biplane called the "Yellow Peril." How that name was assigned was a topic of conversation among the trainees. The "yellow" I could understand because the plane was painted that color. However, the "peril" was something else.

I could not attribute danger, per se, to any aircraft.

For each flight, we needed a flight jacket, gloves, leather helmet with gosport,* and goggles. The instructor was in the front cockpit and the trainee in the rear cockpit. I didn't let the Navy know that I had previous flight training, since word had filtered down to us that the number of washouts was very high among pilots trained beforehand.

I soloed in two weeks. It was a sunny summer morning when the instructor hopped out of the craft and told me to take it up by myself. The air was crystal clear and bright. What a day to solo! But before I could taxi out, he tied a red streamer on my right wing strut. This was standard procedure to let others flying in the vicinity know that a novice was at the controls and "flying high." The familiar head of the instructor was not in sight. I don't remember if I felt any apprehension as I lined up for the take-off, but as I poured the coal to the craft, all feeling of doubt left me and disappeared in the slipstream. I was airborne and on my way. What a feeling to have at my control this many horses compressed into a small radial engine! I already had a private flying license and marvelled at the quick response these added "horses" gave me over fifty-horsepower cubs. The thrill of flying was still there, yet with goggles down and a biplane at my command, I began to imagine the presence of the Red Baron in the vicinity.

I snapped back to reality when the time for my flight ended (too quickly for me!) and eased the throttle back to reduce my altitude as I applied the right rudder and stick pressures to enter the traffic pattern. The name of the game was tail first

---

*A gosport is a *one-way* hollow speaking tube for the instructor to communicate with the student pilot. The instructor spoke into the gosport which brought the sound to the student's ears.

and front wheels second. Any other type of landing would invite a washout. The three-point landing we learned in C.P.T. was taboo. Landing with the throttle fully closed and the tail wheel striking the ground first, followed by the front wheels, assured a complete stall with a minimum distance for the roll-out. It was the Navy way in preparation for carrier landings. Army pilots have ten-thousand-foot runways on which to land. Hence, they can come in "high, hot, and on the wheels" with plenty of runway left after the landing rollout. The reward for soloing was a set of orders transferring me to Corpus Christi. My fellow classmates also took me to Lake Pontchartrain for the traditional, boisterous dunk.

Chapter 5

Training for War

The train ride from New Orleans to Corpus Christi was one I awaited with the anticipation of a young person about to begin world exploration. Failure to be assigned to Pensacola was a blow to my ego, since Pensacola was the ultimate in Naval training bases. Destiny was to prove my Corpus Christi assignment the better one. The West was fascinating to me as mile after mile of the clicking wheels of the train hailed my entrance into the Houston area. I watched the city's skyline grow larger.

The trip from Houston to Corpus Christi kept me anchored to my window seat, hoping to catch sight of roadrunners and other desert creatures. The stunted trees, mesquite brush, and rolling tumbleweed held my attention as I daydreamed, gazing out the window. The fiat country and arroyos every few miles "distorted" the beautiful Texas landscape, but I was being unfair in this value judgment. After all, tourists visiting Louisiana often passed a remark about our trees, saying that they could not see the forest for all the trees in the state.

Dusk was beginning to rise from the Texas ranch lands as we pulled into the Corpus Christi area. I had read so many stories about the ranches located between Corpus Christi and Brownsville, especially the King Ranch, that my anxiety to drink up the culture knew no bounds. I must have portrayed the typical hayseed from the swamps as I stepped off the train.

We were greeted by Navy personnel and a huge cattle car for transportation to the air station. I might add that this form of transportation plagued me on all my military assignments until I reached the rank of full colonel. The sound of fighter engines reached our ears. Most of the advanced flight training syllabus reflecting fighters and dive bombers flown by cadets in the last phases of instruction was held at this main station, because it was good for public relations. The primary and intermediate flights were held at outlying fields near Robstown. Gunnery and bombing runs were on Mustang Island.

We were assigned a full day of ground school classes. The working day would later be split into a morning wing of ground school and an afternoon wing of flight time instructions. Ground school classes reflected the science of flight, celestial navigation, Morse code, aircraft engines, and military protocol. These courses proved to be the nemesis of many cadets. We were given advanced instructions while awaiting flight class assignments. We would hopefully get a grasp of it before cadet status and lessen the washout factor.

These short courses were taught by college professors, hired by the Navy, who came to Corpus Christi from many universities around the country. This training enhanced our chances for success in the program and cut down on military drill during the lag between class assignments. Morse code was easy for me as I had already had a course in radio physics and was well on my way to amateur radio license W5YDC, a license I still hold today.

It might be good here to go over the principle which explains why a plane becomes airborne. The propeller pulls the aircraft through the air. Air current moves over the wings which are shaped in a special way. Air flowing over the upper surface of the wing moves faster than the air flowing underneath, resulting in lower pressure above the wing. This difference in pressure furnishes sufficient lift to sustain an airplane in flight. This is Bernoulli's Principle (increased velocity means a decrease in pressure).

At this time we were not at war with the Axis.* Classes were held and close order drill was stressed as a means of enhancing our status as potential officers. How I hated those drill sessions and the military protocol courses! Surely the higher ranking officers could do better than this! We were not Academy cadets, but potential reserve pilots in for the "duration."

It didn't take long for us to realize the social stratification of military rank. This was especially manifested in the bar which was polarized by three distinct types of officers. The "Ring Knockers," who were Annapolis graduates, stepped up to the bar, and quietly knocked their "forty pound" class ring on it, expecting to be served first. Then there were the reserve officers who made up more than eighty percent of the fighting forces. They dominated the bar. After them came the "Mustang Officers" who started out as enlisted men and made their way up through the ranks to accept officer commissions.

We were given liberty on weekends and wore civilian clothes off base. On my first liberty, I purchased my first and only "Humphrey Bogart" double-breasted suit and a two-staged superheterodyne radio. I was in a different environment and although I missed French music, I enjoyed the Spanish tunes coming over the local frequencies. These fell in phase with my vibrations. Ray-Ban sunglasses with green lenses were the rage

*The Axis powers were Germany, Japan, Italy, and other nations opposing the Allies.

of the Forties. I treasured my pair of gold-rimmed Ray-Bans purchased in downtown Corpus Christi. I "had arrived" and would soon be on flying status. But by the first week of December, there was on the base an air of tension. Word came down that we could no longer keep civilian clothes and must wear our uniforms while on liberty. There went my double-breasted suit. I wore it only once. After the war, the style was out and I had put on a few more pounds.

I received in Corpus Christi another culture shock. I had been born and reared in the bayou country and knew the swamps well. Most of us from Louisiana are bilingual. Although my college transcript reflects Spanish and French, the men with whom I was grouped quickly let me know that in Louisiana one speaks three foreign languages—French, Spanish, *and* English. It was difficult for me to adjust with this group since I had been reared in a Roman Catholic environment and was taunted with words to the effect that Louisiana ranked 48th in the nation in terms of illiteracy and educational standards.*

The military adopted the C.C.C. procedure, initiated by President Roosevelt, of training Southern men in the North and Northern men in the South as a means of healing Civil War wounds. However, all men in aviation were sent south for training because, given the weather, flying is usually handled on a year-round basis. So we were mixed with the "Yankees" in a pool of reserve men waiting to be assigned into a class of one hundred and fifty for the cadet flying program.

To digress for a moment, a certain Lieutenant (jg) Keepers made it miserable for the future cadets in the pool. I venture to

---

*Only in 1959 with the admission of Alaska and Hawaii as the forty-ninth and fiftieth states, respectively, did our country reach the present complement of fifty states.

say that he was hired by the Marine Corps because during his tenure, he turned out more Marine Corps pilots than Navy ones!

The big day finally came on Thursday, October 16, 1941. I was appointed a Naval Aviation cadet, U.S.N.R. (Class 10B 41C) with service number 407 72 04 for pay purposes. We were issued blue identification nameplates* denoting third class cadets.

*Cadets of the intermediate stage held red tags and advanced cadets (upperclassmen) carried white ones.

Chapter 6

The Band Begins to Play

I shall never forget my class of cadets, mostly Yankee football players, English professors, and Ivy Leaguers sprinkled with a few of us Southern boys. It didn't take long before that thin veneer of society wore off the Ivy League boys when we settled down to serious flight training. I was assigned to Ensign Steele, my flight instructor, on December 3, 1941, with aircraft N2S-3, Bureau #4308.

My first flight with Ensign Steele was for orientation. The landscape was different from my Atchafalaya Basin days. The symmetrical patches of sugar cane fields were now replaced with desert landscape under a hot and blazing Texas sun. Ensign Steele told me to relax and let him do the flying. After all, this was my indoctrination flight. I soaked up the flight with visions of roadrunners, cowboys, and gunfights occurring below. This was my cup of tea. The population of Corpus Christi was approximately eighty-six thousand and, from my vantage point, it showed as a sprawled-out Texas town with character. The roads leading out of Corpus Christi were huge bands of pure gold connecting with area towns and disappearing over the horizon into pits of mining towns. Indeed, my imagination was running wild, but was broken after about one half hour of flight when sound waves entered my headset telling me to take the stick and do my thing—not in those words, but in comparable Navy terminology. I flew for about half an hour and managed to keep the plane on a correct course with the horizon in proper position. I had arrived! Ensign Steele didn't say much when we landed, but I knew what he was thinking. He must have sensed that I had already had flight training. I would definitely adapt to Naval aviation.

With the bombing of Pearl Harbor on December 7, 1941, we were at war with Japan. Declarations of war against Italy and Germany followed a couple of days later. Although we sensed that war was imminent, we were nonetheless stunned by the attack. We all felt the impact of President Roosevelt's memorable address in which he called the Japanese assault an "unprovoked and dastardly attack" and the date of the attack a "date that will live in infamy."

The war was no longer chiefly centered in Europe and North Africa, but now encompassed the globe, no part of which could now be described as remote from, or uninvolved in, the conflict. Immediately, the pace of flight training became intensive. The shortage of pilots for the armed forces was a factor in the coming air war. Word came down to accelerate the program and turn out combat pilots.

I soloed again in the required eight hours and was assigned Ensign Gregg as my primary instructor. He carried me through my twenty-hour check flight and I was handed over on December 21 to Ensign Varne for my check flight test. I got an "up" and was sent on January 10, 1942, to Ensign Curran for night flying instructions.

Night flying was a different ball game. The cockpit of the N3N-3 was "strange" to me. Gone were the familiar instruments glaring brightly under the intensity of the sun and naked switches exposed and easily activated. Instrument dials became glowing infrared eyes daring you to recognize them, much less understand what messages they were trying to relay to your brain. To compound the situation, switches which were familiar in daylight were now located only by the Braille method, which had to be done with finesse lest you throw the wrong switch.

As if this were not enough, we were warned about instrument conditions, a phase which should have been introduced before this night flying training period! "Keep your eyes open and watch the lights ahead of you" were the rules of the game. But nothing was said about the possibility of confusing the lights of another plane and a bright star. Some cadets followed a star they believed to be the lights of a plane ahead of them until their own plane ran out of fuel. The exhaust pipes looked cool in the daytime, but at night, visible sheets of flame coming out of them gave the false impression that the plane was on fire. One cadet bailed out, believing his plane to be on fire. A few cadets landed their planes on top of each other, causing a few deaths of instructors and students alike. Many developed vertigo and simply flew into the ground. Yes, night flying had its hazards. As it was, rules and regulations in aviation were often made as direct beneficial consequences of these terrible tragedies.

My love for flying helped me breeze through this phase. I had no trouble with the instruments and the night gauges. Excellent 20/10 eyesight gave me an edge since I could land the craft regardless of ground fog haze or diffused glare produced by landing lights. I felt I could actually feel the location of the ground before I landed. I comfortably soloed the same night after going through the procedures.

The next flight check would be the thirty-three-hour one.

This would be acrobatics and precision flying. A period which proved to be a cadet's nightmare was for me almost routine. I was never airsick in my entire flying career and I looked forward to acrobatic flying. The short-field dead stick landing phase proved my first stumbling block. With Ensign Gregg as my instructor, I had no trouble and shot good patterns during the morning instructions. In the afternoon, I was up for a check along with three other cadets. We all hit the assigned circle patterns, but downwind. We failed to note that the wind had shifted 180 degrees since the morning action and as a result all four of us received a "down" for the test. The next day, we breezed through the test with flying colors and completed the Navy's primary flight course. We were then assigned to Phase II, intermediate training using monoplanes having more horsepower.

This phase involved the mathematics of steep flight turns. My old physics days really paid off here. The mathematics of a steep turn fascinated me. I arrived at the following conclusions. (1) The slower the plane, the faster it turns. (2) A faster plane cannot turn as rapidly as a slower one and a twin-engined craft cannot turn as rapidly as a single-engined one. (3) You cannot increase the turn by kicking rudder or by pulling back on the stick. (4) To increase the turn, you must increase the bank. (5) As the bank increases, the wing loading and load factor increase. At 60 degrees, for instance, you weigh twice as much, regardless of how fast you may be flying.

For intermediate training, I reported to another field in the Corpus Christi area and was assigned SNV-1, Bureau #003006 (Vultee Vibrator), a monoplane. Ensign Clem was my instructor. This aircraft had landing flaps, radio, and an enclosed cockpit. With 450 horsepower strapped to me, I felt drunk with power. I soloed right after my checkout run of one and a half hours. During this phase, I had Ensigns Collins, Clem, Looney, and Cline as instructors. The instruments and radio flight checks were a piece of cake and I completed the requirements without difficulty. I always felt comfortable on instruments. I was checked by Ensigns Weyland, Dreyer, and Hendricks and cleared for advanced flight training, the last phase.

On March 24, 1942, I was assigned to the fighter field for fighter pilot instructions. My dream had come true. I received a checkout in the SNC-1, Bureau #6337, with Lieutenant (jg) Dose. After this day, I was on my own. There would be no more in-flight instructors or passengers. Communications would be by radio. By March 31, I had logged 146 hours of flight training and on April 17, I hopped into the very fighter I had seen at the movies, the F3F-3, a Navy fighter of the Thirties. I was in the cockpit of Bureau #1925, a fighter with over 1200 horsepower, having two forward-firing machine guns synced through the propeller, with the firing mechanism attached to the control stick.

I cannot describe the thrill I felt as I poured the coal to the little Grumman biplane. The plane leaped into the air in seconds and it took me just a few more seconds to control all those "horses" running wild under the cowling. I flew the familiarization hop for half an hour, doing the usual maneuvers, but my thoughts were on the machine gun levers hanging on the control stick. I even looked into the gunsight and could "see" the Red Baron ahead of me. Two levers had to be jackknifed parallel with the control stick before firing the guns. One controlled the .50-caliber machine gun, the other controlled the .30-caliber one. Both guns fired through the propeller. But the revolutions of the propeller had to be above 1,000 rpms or there would be danger of shooting it off. A telescopic tubular gunsight penetrated the windscreen. It must have been quite a task to fly and fight at the same time. If you failed to fly smoothly and were skidding slightly, the machine gun bullets would take off on a tangent to your flight path and you would miss the target. Hence, smooth flying during training was emphasized. As cadets, we learned to ignore this obsolete gunsight and fired the guns at the towed sleeve by "feel." We got more hits this way. The gunnery phase passed with little trouble for most of us. Those who failed this part were taken out of fighters and placed in twin-engined aircraft or dive bombers.

Next came carrier landings. One had to obtain eight satisfactory approaches and landings on a small field having a fixed carrier deck painted on the runway. A signal officer on the deck would pick us up in the approach pattern and control our flight attitude with two signal paddles held in his hands.*

It was this phase that nearly cost me my life, or if I survived, my flying career. On the morning of Sunday, April 19, 1942, we were practicing right hand turns onto the simulated carrier deck. I had successfully completed four landings and was going around for my fifth approach. Four pilots were in the landing

---

*If your approach was too high, the officer would hold his paddles above his head and would lower them as you corrected your flight approach. If you were too slow or near stalling speed, he would give you a come-on signal by scooping the paddles in front of his body. This would remind you to apply more throttle. If you were coming in too fast and incorrectly, he would wave you off with a frantic cross of his arms which meant for you to go around and try another approach. If all were okay, he would bring you in with arms outstretched and level with his shoulders. When your plane was almost adjacent to him, he would make one motion across his throat with his right hand, as a signal to chop the throttle and land the aircraft. This would be the signal to catch a wire with your tail hook and come to a halt aboard the carrier. Of course after the cut, we would land and then push the throttle forward and go around for another try, leaving the runway ready for the next plane in the landing pattern.

pattern practicing this phase of instructions.

As I made my approach for the fifth time, I was in the correct position, a few knots above stalling speed, and was receiving an okay from the signal officer. I suddenly felt the little fighter begin to sink. The officer gave me the signal to apply power since my fighter was about to stall. I applied the necessary action, but the fighter didn't respond. By this time, I was about forty feet up and adjacent to the signal officer when the craft stalled and fell out of the air in a spin. The right wing and engine struck the runway and turned the aircraft 180 degrees, skidding down the runway in a reverse landing. The wheels were wiped out. By reflex, I cut the engine switch to prevent any fire from breaking out. My goggles were down when my head smashed into the gunsight, shattering one of the lens. We did not have shoulder straps in those days, only lap belts. The instructor rushed to pull me out of the cockpit, believing I was a dead man, but I was already out on the wing by the time he arrived. One of the cadets following me described the accident and kidded me about the backwards landing.

A board convened in my case, but I was released for flying duty again when all the facts were presented. I had four straight okays. The reason the plane didn't respond was due to a faulty throttle linkage in my fighter. The Flight Surgeon related my calm attitude when he checked my eyes and limbs after the crash. By April 25, I was flying again and was assigned F3F-3 Bureau #1453.

The weather worsened in May, so most of my class received little flying time. Although graduation was delayed, most of us met all of the requirements by the end of June. Then came the bombshell. Our class had been earmarked for P-Boats (reconnaissance aircraft). It appeared that there was in the fleet a shortage of search pilots. Some were needed immediately as the war against the Japanese was not going well. With only 228 hours of flight time and a few hours of gunnery, I wanted to remain in fighters.

The officer in charge of complaints stated simple Navy procedure. If you wanted fighters or dive bombers and if you were in the top fifteen percent of the graduating class, you could transfer to the Marine Corps and get your wish, provided they accepted you. I had no real knowledge of the Marine Corps except that they were always in the news. I had no other option and was glad to join the Marines. I signed up that very day, July 2, 1942. I was appointed a second lieutenant in the Reserves and assigned to Marine Barracks, NAS, Corpus Christi, with a fifteen-day leave before being assigned to the Naval Air Station in San Diego.

* * * *

It was refreshing to be in St. Martinville again. By this time, most of the young men had been drafted and were in training. It was nice to dress in Marine Corps whites with wings of gold and brand new second lieutenant bars on my shoulders. I dated Louise and when we attended functions and movies, the expense tab was picked up by the townsmen. I recalled Rudyard Kipling's *Tommy,* a poem I had read in one of my college English classes taught by Muriel McCollough.

> O it's Tommy this, an' Tommy that, an' "Tommy go away";
> But it's "Thank you, Mister Atkins," when the band begins to play. . . .*

*"The band begins to play" is a British expression which refers to the outbreak of war.

My comrades and I knew Kipling's poetry very well. Later, we would often change the words of his poems to fit our situation in the war we were fighting. Kipling was truly an inspiration to me.

Chapter 7

The Wild West

My first set of orders as an officer reflected assignment to the Advanced Carrier Training Group (ACTG) at San Diego. Late one evening, I hopped aboard a train in Lafayette for the trip to California. I quickly located my sleeping berth and was off to bed for the night, sleeping through the entire state of Texas. I was up at daybreak and went to the diner. I selected a seat near a window and had a quiet breakfast and coffee while "drinking in" the view. We had just departed El Paso and were heading for Las Cruces and Lordsberg, New Mexico, when I got the strangest feeling that I had been here before. This was my cup of tea. To this day, the stretch from El Paso to Las Cruces holds a power over me that I cannot shake. Later on, whenever I pulled active reserve summer duty in El Toro, California, my family and I traveled this route in our car. The West began to unfold before my eyes as I sipped my morning coffee and enjoyed the scenery. What a peaceful setting! I looked forward with renewed vigor to my West Coast adventure.

When we reached the Sierra Nevada Mountains, we had to wait an hour on a siding for another engine to arrive and help the train overcome the grade as we entered the steep slope of those mountains. By 2300 hours (11:00 PM), we were on the station platform in Los Angeles. A switch had to be made for the run into San Diego. We were on our way within thirty minutes and a few hours later we entered Union Station in San Diego which was in total darkness since the West Coast was on wartime alert.

As luck would have it, I ran into Jug Herlihy who was wearing a uniform similar to mine. I had not seen him since he left Corpus Christi to go to Pensacola, electing to fly dive bombers. Our common denominator was the Marine Corps. You guessed it: a cattle car was there to transport us to the dock for water transportation to North Island. We crossed the deep channel in total darkness. It was only when the sun rose that we were able to enjoy the plush surroundings of this California base.

The following day was foggy. It would take a few weeks to become acclimated to the environment of the West Coast. Orientation was the order of the day, which I hastened to get behind me as quickly as possible. Flight time was the name of the game and I certainly intended to get my share. The sun usually burned through the fog and haze by 1000 hours (10:00 AM). I looked forward to a familiarization hop that very morning.

We were given the SNJ-3, an aircraft having 600 horsepower. This was a craft used to get flight pay since we were not yet assigned to a fighter squadron. Eager to get as much flight time as possible, I went to photo school, which was duly noted in my service record. As you will see later on in this narrative, this would come back to haunt me! (I learned the hard way—never volunteer!)

Our ACTG training resulted in a high mortality rate among newly commissioned pilots. More pilots were killed here than in combat. One of the casualties was Lieutenant Freddie Gross, a friend of mine. He would talk a lot about his father who was a Marine Corps pilot during World War I. He had a big globe and anchor on the radiator of his sports car of which he was proud. We had just completed our photo mission when Freddie joined a group of other pilots in a tail chase. This SNJ-3 was red lined at 250 knots, which meant that if you were to fly the craft at this speed in a dive, you had to be certain that the wings were level with respect to the horizon in the pull-out. The pilot must pull out of the dive with the least amount of G forces on the wings or they would pull off. It appears that during one of the maneuvers, Freddie pulled out beyond the red line mark with one wing below the horizon. A wing came off and the plane went straight into the ground. Lieutenant John McEniry, Jr.,* another friend of mine, escorted the body back to Lonoke, Arkansas.

* * * *

While at North Island in that summer of 1942, I went to the Navy docks and noticed a submarine moored. As this was the first time I had seen a sub, I was very curious and went over to talk with the officers near the conning tower. The skipper noticedT my wings and laughingly asked me to take him up in a plane. I agreed provided he would let aboard the sub! Needless to say, we had a nice flight followed by an interesting tour of the U.S.S. *Wahoo.***

*In later years, Colonel John Howard McEniry, Jr., wrote his book, *A Marine Dive-Bomber Pilot at Guadalcanal.* He is now deceased.

**Medal of Honor recipient Rear Admiral Richard H. O'Kane inscribed for me a copy of his book, *Wahoo: The Patrols of America's Most Famous World War II Submarine* (Novato, CA: Presidio Press, 1987). Little did I realize that I was walking into history when I stepped aboard the *Wahoo.*

Chapter 8

G-8 Remembered

On September 28, 1942, I checked out in the Grumman Wildcat fighter, F4F-3, Bureau #02036,* and was assigned on October 2 to Marine Fighting Squadron 112. The transition from beautiful living quarters on North Island to the dusty field quarters of VMF-112 at Kearney Mesa was a drag. Like a king, I had been living with liberty galore on North Island! Now I was in a tent somewhere in the boondocks, eating peanut butter and jelly for breakfast. What a letdown! The mess hall was screened and our dining tables were field-equipped wooden ones. There was one long runway without a control tower.

Major Paul Fontana was our commanding officer at this time. As I was introduced to the Major, I sensed my failure to make a good impression because his facial expression changed when I said, in answer to his question, that I was from Louisiana. To compound this, I was assigned his aircraft for my familiarization flight. Time was a factor and combat training

*The F4F Wildcat was the Navy's standard fighter at the beginning of the war. Inferior to the Zero (Japanese fighter plane), it nevertheless held the line until better planes were produced. The Wildcat's armament consisted of six .50-caliber machine guns mounted in the wings. On some models, bombs or rockets were carried beneath the wings for special missions. The range could be extended by the use of two droppable 50-gallon tanks suspended from the wings near the fuselage. The wings could also be folded manually for compact storage on carriers. A hand crank in the cockpit retracted the landing gear.

was in high gear. This led us to be negligent in such things as reading manuals for new aircraft. "Fly one, you can fly them all" was the going doctrine, so I hopped into the Major's plane, taxied out, and took off. I'll hand it to Lee Roy Grumman. The Wildcat was a beautifully, structurally stable, and, therefore, excellent carrier plane and gun platform from which to shoot. I climbed to 12,000 feet and went through fighter tactics to get the feel of the plane.

As I was preparing to return to base, I noticed that the radio compass wasn't functioning. I remembered that G-8 and his Flying Aces from the comic books always struck the instruments a few times if they didn't work so that is what I did. The compass needle remained motionless, though I succeeded in breaking the glass. Upon landing, I taxied back to the line, grabbed the yellow sheet,* and jotted down in beautiful language my comments about the sticky gauge. The plane captain, upon reading the sheet, asked if I had turned on the switch controlling the compass. I turned four colors and mumbled a few choice words. From then on, I read manuals before checking out in new aircraft. I'm sure that Major Fontana was notified of this little incident.

Before I could accumulate more time with the squadron, we were ordered overseas. I did not have any gunnery or night flying experience in the fighter I was going to fly into combat a few weeks later. *C'est la guerre!* That's war! We struck camp and began loading equipment for the overseas tour. On October 10, 1942, we boarded a Lurline liner in San Diego harbor. Just before sailing time, Lieutenant Jack Maas, a pilot with an I.Q.

---

*The yellow sheet is a document all pilots fill out. The plane captain hands the pilot the yellow sheet for him to sign and thus accept the craft as flight worthy. Upon his return, the pilot jots down on the same yellow sheet any malfunctions or troubles encountered during flight.

of 9,000 coupled with a sixth sense, decided that we needed shoulder holsters for our .45-caliber automatic pistols, the standard-issue sidearm for all U.S. military officers.* If you had to bail out with the gun strapped around your waist, neither the belt nor the gun would survive the parachute opening. Twenty-five of our pilots got shoulder holsters costing a few dollars each and made by a gunsmith Jack knew in San Diego. I still have my holster.

*Firing a heavy, brush-cutting bullet, the colt .45-caliber automatic pistol was especially useful as a jungle-fighting weapon.

Chapter 9

Under the Southern Cross

The trip to the war zone was an experience for this old boy from the swamps. All through our navigational courses, we worked star sites and problems reflecting the skies of the Northern hemisphere on the Greenwich side of the International Date Line. This was a new ball game. The constellations of the Southern hemisphere and the time zone in terms of days, not hours, were the rules. From the darkened deck of the ship, we saw the Big Dipper which was inverted on the horizon. Of course, the North Star was completely "under water" and would remain so until our return to the States.* The Southern Cross would be our friend along with Orion whose belt of three stars marked the dividing line between the Northern and Southern hemispheres, the celestial equator.

A compulsory "crossing the line" initiation was held, during which we were transformed from pollywogs to shellbacks: kissing

*All large, massive objects in the universe are spherical, such as the sun, stars, and planets. The force of gravity increases with decreasing altitude and vice-versa. When an object gains mass, the gravity increases until it compresses around a central point. Thus, there is a sphere equally enclosing a center. By the laws of physics, it can't be any other shape! Also, the force of gravity for objects on the surface is less than the gravitational attraction for such objects because the centrifugal force caused by the rotation tends to counteract the gravitational effect. That's why we're not smashed on the surface of the spherical Earth!

the belly of King Neptune's baby (a greasy, fat man in a diaper and baby bonnet), crawling through garbage, being beaten with bats, etc.! That's how it's always been done. However, ours was toned-down because of wartime alert.

I was fortunate not to be seasick and enjoyed every minute of our voyage. The nights were superb. The stars stood out like bright jewels, brilliantly defying their assigned order of magnitude. We crammed in a Southern hemisphere course along with the possibility of three Sundays in a week relative to the International Date Line.

The ship clipped along at a fast 22 knots and we soon docked at Noumea, New Caledonia. Since we had no knowledge of our destination, the area was a total mystery for most of us. It was only when I was called to my commanding officer's quarters that I became aware of New Caledonia as a French-mandated island. Since I was from Louisiana and could speak French, I was selected to be among the first ashore as an interpreter. The expressions on the faces of my Ivy League colleagues made my day as I walked with an aristocratic gait down the gangplank. I really rubbed it in!

Noumea reminded me of Louisiana. I felt at home on its streets. The voices speaking French were pleasant sounds as I could understand it all and read the street signs. Maybe my C.O. forgave my breaking his compass glass as we walked the streets of Noumea. The extent of my interpretations was in terms of our location ashore as a squadron and a possible aux- iliary site for an airfield. It's funny how the thin veneer of society's culture breaks down among strangers when one speaks the language. I thought I would receive from the mayor a key to the "city." (Only later did I come to under- stand that the Vichy government of metropolitan France, which was sympathetic to Nazi Germany, was trying to assert its authority over French overseas territories in opposition to the Free French movement of General Charles de Gaulle who was our ally.) Before the troops disembarked, we walked to the top of a cliff overlooking the harbor where eighteenth century gun emplacements were located. Like kids, we wrote our names, ranks, and serial numbers on the roster at the site.

We had hardly settled down to tropical tent living, when Major Fontana called the pilots into his tent area and asked for four volunteers to fly with him the next day to Cactus, the code name for Guadalcanal, an island in the Solomon chain, northeast of Australia. This was November 2, 1942, and replacements were needed to fill in the losses in combat. It was then that we realized we would not fight right away as a squadron unit, but as replacement pilots. Little did we suspect that pilots were available, but only a few fighters were in commission. I volunteered (I didn't know better at the time), stating I was the only pilot new to his squadron with the least amount of time. He turned me down. That damn compass again! I felt I was not a true member of VMF-112, having transferred to the unit just prior to its shipping out.

On the last evening before leaving the ship in Noumea, we had a Catholic Mass for the men going into combat. I volunteered as an altar boy along with another pilot, Lieutenant Le Blanc from Minnesota. After the services, we compared our French backgrounds. He didn't speak French. Unfortunately, he didn't survive the year. A dive-bomber pilot, he was killed in the line of duty sometime in December.*

---

*"De Blanc" is French for "of white." Le Blanc, as in Lieutenant Le Blanc and the currently popular young actor Matt Le Blanc, means "the white."

Chapter 10

The Dark Days of 1942

It might be well at this point to reflect on the causes of our defensive action on Guadalcanal. By the middle of 1942, the Japanese had occupied a vast area encompassing the western Pacific (including Wake Island and, in Alaska, the islands of Attu and Kiska), eastern China, French Indochina, the Philippines, Singapore, the Dutch East Indies, and much of the island of New Guinea. Their strategy was to thrust eastward to threaten Hawaii and the American west coast and, at the same time, southeastward in order to isolate Australia. General Douglas MacArthur fled the Philippines shortly before it fell, publicly vowing, "I shall return!" He became the Commander of Forces in the Southwest Pacific.

The Doolittle raid on Tokyo (April 18, 1942) galvanized American morale. This was much needed at the time. The raid also convinced Admiral Isoroku Yamamoto of the vulnerability of the Japanese mainland. Yamamoto also lost face because his job was to protect the emperor!

The Battle of the Coral Sea (May 4 to 8) turned back the Japanese invasion forces destined for Port Moresby in Papua. Admiral Frank J. Fletcher commanded our ships and planes during this battle in which all the fighting was in the air.

The Battle of Midway (June 4 to 7) stopped Japanese expansion eastward. Admiral Chester W. Nimitz, Pacific Fleet Commander, and Rear Admirals Frank J. Fletcher and Raymond A. Spruance directed our forces in that battle.

Now we were still on the defensive in the Pacific. President Franklin D. Roosevelt had agreed with British Prime Minister Winston Churchill, during their conferences in Washington, D.C., in December of 1941, that Germany would have to be defeated first. The preponderance of effort and supplies would consequently be in the European and North African theatres. This left the Pacific theatre operating on a shoestring budget and with a dearth of materials for our fighting men selected to stem the tide of the Japanese.

In May of 1942, the Japanese seized Tulagi, the British administrative capital of the Solomon Islands. Soon thereafter, they began to construct an airfield near Lunga Point on the nearby island of Guadalcanal. The significance of this airfield was apparent. The noose around Australia was beginning to tighten!

On August 7, 1942, U.S. Marines, led by General Alexander A. Vandegrift, landed at Red Beach on Guadalcanal. The Japanese airfield was captured the next day. It was hurriedly finished with construction equipment the Japanese had left behind. The airfield was christened "Henderson Field," after Major Lofton R. Henderson, a Marine dive-bomber squadron leader who was killed during the Battle of Midway. On August 20, the Cactus Air Force was born when carrier-based Wildcats and dive bombers arrived in Guadalcanal. Brigadier General Roy Stanley Geiger, commander of Marine Air Wing One, directed the air defense of our forces.

The Battle of Guadalcanal was a defensive one. During the latter part of 1942 and into 1943, the Japanese attempted to recapture Henderson Field with the support of air and naval forces. The ships of Admiral Tanaka's "Tokyo Express" would arrive in the Slot during the nighttime hours to shell Henderson Field and leave so as to be out of range of our fighters and dive bombers when daylight came. While we owned the day, the nights belonged to the Japanese. And what long and harrowing nights they were!

On August 21, Japanese troops commanded by Colonel Kiyoano Ichiki attempted to recapture Henderson Field via Alligator Creek about a half mile from Fighter One (the cow pasture, near Henderson Field, which became a fighter airfield). They were defeated by Lieutenant Colonel Edwin A. Pollock's Marines. On August 24, the Naval Battle of the Eastern Solomons was fought with losses on both sides.

Other Japanese attacks on September 13 and 14 resulted in the Battle of Bloody Ridge during which Lieutenant Colonel Merritt A. Edson's Raiders (1st Marine Raider Battalion) defeated General Kiyotaki Kawaguchi's forces. Bloody Ridge was about one and a half miles from Fighter One and was the spot from which "Pistol Pete" (more on him later) fired mortars on us as we took off on flights.

U.S. infantrymen wore the standard drab green uniform with the G.I.'s steel helmet, a versatile item that protected the head in combat and could serve as a pot for heating water and rations when the fighting died down. Each soldier carried the M-1 Garand semiautomatic rifle, which armed the majority of U.S. infantry troops during World War II. It was a superb weapon prized for its ruggedness, reliability, and relatively high rate of fire. The bayonet, carried on the belt, could be fitted to the rifle. This edged weapon still had a place in modern warfare especially in the brutal hand-to-hand combat on Guadalcanal. This was especially so during the Battle of Bloody Ridge before I arrived.

I didn't know very much about the infantry's heavier weapons except that the machine guns were mainly .50-caliber (like the ones in my plane's wings) and their tanks had thicker armor than Japanese tanks. The Japanese tanks were so thin skinned that our tanks and artillery would blow large, ragged holes in them. But this is beyond the scope of my book. Readers interested in these aspects of the Guadalcanal campaign may read some other books written about the conflict.

On September 21, 1942, Admiral Aubrey Fitch assumed command of land-based air forces in the South Pacific, replacing Admiral J. S. McCain. On October 18, Admiral William F. "Bull" Halsey, Jr. assumed the South Pacific command.

Admiral Yamamoto and General Harukichi Hyakutake planned for the middle of October yet another offensive to take Henderson Field. This Japanese attempt, executed on October 24 and 25, failed after much bitter fighting on both sides.

On November 12 through 15, the Naval Battle of Guadalcanal took place with air and sea engagements off Cape Esperance and Tassafaronga Point. The Japanese failed yet again.

On December 9, General Vandegrift and his men left for a well-deserved rest in Australia. He was relieved by Army General Alexander M. Patch. There would be much action during December and January. But the battle for Guadalcanal was over by early February 1943.

United States and Allied casualties on land, sea, and air included some 7,100 killed and permanently missing during the Battle of Guadalcanal. Japanese soldiers, airmen, and sailors who lost their lives numbered at least 30,000. There were some forty-three native islander deaths resulting from the battle.*

*Richard B. Frank, *Guadalcanal: The Definitive Account of the Landmark Battle* (New York: Penguin, 1992), pp. 613-14.

Finally, mention must be made of the coastwatchers who were our eyes and ears during the action in the Solomons and without whom the battle would surely have been lost. Admiral Halsey summed up their contribution when he said, "The coastwatchers saved Guadalcanal, and Guadalcanal saved the Pacific."* But it was a close call!

*Quoted by coastwatcher John Keenan in an Anzac Day speech (April 25, 1995) and another speech that is undated. Halsey's statement is also quoted by Phyllis Keenan in her prologue to her husband's book, Lieutenant Commander John Robert Keenan, *Diary of a Coast Watcher from October 1942 to February 1943* (Aspley, Queensland, Australia: Keenan Family Trust, 1998), p 3.

PART TWO

WHEN THE WORLD WAS YOUNG

The world was young
and
we knew we would never die!

Captain William "Tex" Jordan
Texas Border Patrol
VMF-113 Intelligence Officer
Author of *No Second Place Winner*

Chapter 11

VMF-112 in the Cactus Air Force

The Marine Corps MATS transport unit flew the remaining VMF-112 pilots from New Caledonia to Guadalcanal on November 10.* Upon landing on the cow pasture dirt field called Fighter One, we were rushed on jeeps to the tent area under palm trees near the shoreline about a half mile from the field. Henderson Field held only dive bombers and heavy transport aircraft, which needed special reinforced runways. We were issued strip aerial maps of the Solomon Islands Slot with the names of the various islands superimposed. We were to study the map and would be scheduled for a familiarization flight that very day.

On my first flight, I accompanied Lieutenant Bill Marontate, a pilot from Joe Foss' division in Major Duke Davis' squadron. Bill pointed out the various landmarks while I checked the oxygen mask and blowers on the little fighter. We were fired upon by Japanese troops as we landed, a factor that was considered a fringe benefit by the fighter pilots of the Cactus Air Force as we were called. We were always under fire on take-offs and landings so we used a carrier-approach type of landing to avoid small arms fire, the "fringe benefit"!

*I am indebted to the staff writers of Pocket Books for their helpful revision of some of the material in my book, which was published in *Top Guns: America's Fighter Aces Tell Their Stories* (New York: Pocket Books, 1991). I have used some of their revisions in the present text.

53

It took this gunfire to make me realize just how close we were to the front lines. We held only the airstrips and were protected on the perimeter by Marine ground troops. We could not leave the tents at night for any reason, because Japanese infantrymen would infiltrate during the nighttime hours. Marine guards, located in fixed firing positions with rifles ready, would shoot anything that moved. Toilet facilities were indeed a problem, but could be handled under these conditions.

By sunset on that first day I had become familiar with the flying area and the Solomon slot map. I could hardly believe my eyes, and felt as if I were home in the Atchafalaya Basin. The names of most of these islands in the Solomon chain were French and Spanish. Both languages were common in Louisiana, and I could speak each fairly fluently. This was a good omen for me, and I felt that the world was young and I would never die here. I could survive in the jungles of this island chain if I were forced down. That this was a home away from home gave me an added edge of confidence in the air combat battles which followed.

We were awake before dawn and had a breakfast of hardtack and C rations with "coffee" to wash it down. Since only a few fighters were in commission, the flights were rotated among many pilots from different squadrons. I missed the dawn patrol of two fighters, but got in the eleven o'clock daily action over Henderson Field. It was my first combat action and also my first view of death in the skies. I had been assigned as number-four man in Lieutenant Marontate's fighter division, and as such flew wing on Staff Sergeant Joe Palko. Joe was an experienced, smooth-flying pilot, yet I would witness his death that very day.

Fighter Command managed to get ten F4F-3 Wildcats airborne before a flight of fifteen Japanese twin-engined Betty bombers reached the airfield. This was an almost daily affair and, unknown to me at this time, coastwatchers up the chain of islands would radio these flights to us. This would give us the altitude advantage on the Japanese planes. It is axiomatic with fighter pilots that the man with the altitude advantage generally wins all the marbles. We were climbing through 10,000 feet and heading up to 25,000 feet when we spotted the enemy bombers at about 15,000 feet, starting in on a bombing run on Henderson Field. We didn't have the altitude advantage and had to get that position before beginning a firing overhead run on the bombers. I could not see the advantage of this maneuver that we had been taught in flight school and were now using in combat. These were World War I tactics that would leave us at a disadvantage against enemy fighters, but second lieutenants simply follow orders. My duty was to fly wing on Joe Palko and follow through the firing run on the bombers while protecting Joe's tail against enemy fighters. In the first overhead pass we dropped two bombers on fire but failed to scatter the others that were already locked in their bombing run.

I believe today that a head-on run would have dropped more bombers, scattering them from the bombing run and giving us the position to cut off their escape, if some managed to complete the run. We went by the book, the Japanese dropped the bombs after our first pass, and were on their way home before we could get a second pass. Our division of four planes went after the two crippled bombers. One was immediately blown up in the air by our first two fighters. The other one, still on fire, was heading for the Japanese-held island of Tulagi. I could not see the wisdom of attacking a crippled bomber that could do no harm with its bomb load, but followed Joe Palko and the others down toward it. I scanned the skies for enemy fighters, but saw none and radioed this information to the others.

Joe started a high-side run on the flaming bomber and I followed, only to see another fighter making the same type of run from the other side! Before I could pick up the mike to yell a warning, I watched in horror as both Grumman fighters began firing at the crippled bomber at the same time as its rear gunner opened up with his 20mm cannons, concentrating on Joe's fighter. To this day, I don't know if Joe was hit by gunfire, or if it was the slight collision of the two fighters as they flew past the tail of the bomber. That may have knocked out Joe momentarily. I saw a flash of fire and one of the pilots bailing out. It was Lieutenant Pedersen from the other fighter. I followed Joe down, and it looked like he had control of his fighter, but at the last minute, he crashed on the beach of Tulagi. I marked the spot on my knee-pad map and also the spot where Lieutenant Pedersen landed in the water. Then I went after the Japanese bomber, but it was too late. The pilot landed the burning aircraft in a lagoon among friendly Japanese forces.

Back at Henderson Field I was told to report to Captain Joe Foss. I briefed him on what happened, and he immediately took off in a J2F float plane to search for Palko and Pedersen. I was ready for coffee and a rest and prayed that Joe Palko was all right, but he did not survive. Pedersen was picked up and returned to the field. I will never forget that first, vivid action. I had fired on a bomber and put a few holes in it, but failed to bring it down. I will always remember this first action as we flew alongside the Japanese bomber stream, climbing for position to make a firing run. I could see the Japanese rear gunners swing their guns around toward us as we climbed out of range. Forever etched in my mind is the flaming Japanese bomber and the death of Joe Palko.

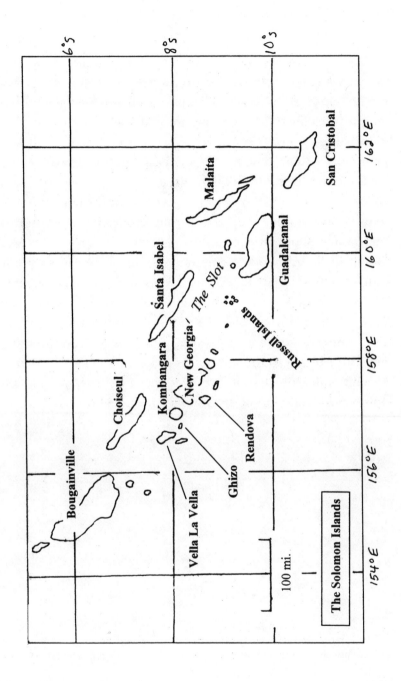

The Solomon Islands

I lay awake on my cot with the sounds of ten thousand mosquitos trying to penetrate the mosquito netting, somehow hoping to rationalize the three-plane formation flying we were taught in cadet training. These were World War I tactics that didn't apply here. Contradictorily, we were told to scissor-maneuver with our enemy in a dogfight, but here in combat we were instructed not to dogfight the highly maneuverable Zero fighters!* Later, from my combat experiences, I was in a position to understand. It appeared that about eighty percent of the fighter pilots on each side stuck with the ways they were taught in flight school. Come hell or high water, many pilots trained to follow a certain pattern will fly that way in combat— the same throttle settings, the same smooth climbing turn, the same breakaway regardless of any dogfighting they may do. This training pattern is easy to note, and easy to lead with gunfire. But I began to think in terms of aggressive fighter tactics, with an outlet for survival. I realized that I would have to develop my own tactics in order to survive in the Solomons!

---

*Although outperformed by other fighters, the F4F Wildcat proved to be a very durable aircraft due to its rugged construction which kept it flying even after many enemy hits. It had extra armor and a self-sealing fuel tank.

Chapter 12

The Big Naval Battle of November 12 to 15

My second air battle was on November 12, 1942. This time I flew with members of my own squadron. Major Fontana, our skipper, was scheduled to lead a flight of eight fighters for the eleven o'clock daily action. I was one of the eight and would fly wing on Lieutenant James L. Secrest. I was low man on the totem pole in terms of flight hours, hence my position as wingman for a while. This soon changed, and I would be leading flights as the war progressed.

Captain Joe Foss had eight fighters at Angels 25 (25,000 feet) flying early patrol when "Condition Red" sounded and we scrambled. Our first four fighters off the deck created a cloud of dust that enabled the Japanese mortar expert, nicknamed "Pistol Pete," to get a fix on the runway. My group of four took off through a barrage of bursting mortar shells. I didn't pick up any arrows from this fire as I cleared the coconut trees at the end of the runway and climbed for altitude, banking sharply over our fleet off the shore of Guadalcanal. As we passed through 5000 feet, Major Fontana's voice crackled in my earphones, directing our attention to the AA fire from the fleet below.

Looking down at the fleet, I saw fifteen or more twin-engined Betty torpedo bombers coming around the 'Canal and starting a high-speed run on the fleet at about fifty feet. They were in the

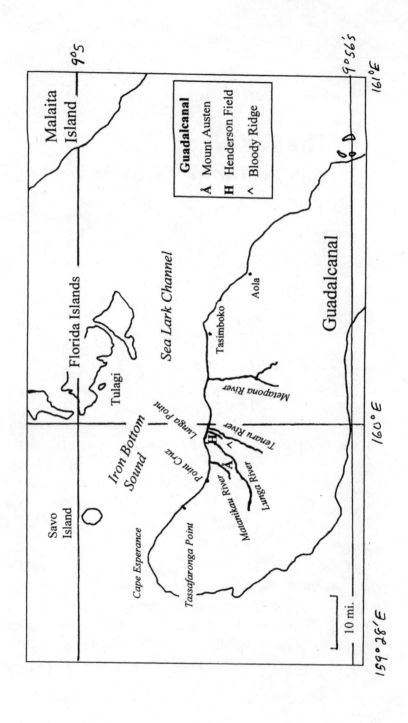

most perfectly strung-out run I have ever seen, and this time we had the advantage. It was a fighter pilot's dream. The altitude was ours and we would not have to compensate for speed and position, just dive on the sitting ducks below us. Under no circumstances would I ever be a bomber pilot in combat! Our fleet was at a disadvantage. They could not maneuver to avoid the bombers, and had difficulty in lowering the deck guns from the "up" position to the "down" position at the water line for firing purposes. Regardless, they were sending up a huge barrage of antiaircraft fire that we had to fly through.

Joe Foss and his flight had spotted the Japanese bombers and were on the way down from 25,000 feet to engage them. My flight dived through the AA fire, and two of our fighters were hit and crashed into the ocean.* Then we hit the enemy bombers at high speed. The action was too fast and fierce for fear to catch up with me. I flew through the barrage from the fleet and locked onto the tail of a Betty and opened fire, killing the rear gunner and watching my tracers strike the engines. The plane burst into flames immediately, and I almost flew into the bomber due to target fixation. I was awed by the winding down of its two engines' propellers as seen through my own propeller turning at greater revolutions. The stroboscopic effect was hypnotic. Flying through the heat generated by the flaming bomber, I quickly recovered and locked onto the tail of another bomber, adjacent to me at about fifty feet off the water. I sent this one crashing in flames with a short burst of the six .50-caliber machine guns.**

*Though seriously wounded, both pilots (Lieutenant W. W. Wamel and Staff Sergeant Tom Hurst) survived and eventually recovered.

**Forty-six years later I found out that I had "flown through" the gunsight of SM1 Don H, Dahlke aboard the destroyer *Fletcher*. Don had just shot down a Betty bomber and was focusing on another when he noted an out-of-place Marine Wildcat fighter in his gunsight. Several rounds left his 20mm cannon before he could check his reflexes. I did not get hit from this fire. Admiral Bull Halsey awarded the Silver Star to Don for his action that day. I'm glad that I wasn't part of his citation!

I had cleared the fleet by this time, knowing that there were other bombers coming out of their runs and clearing the fleet as well. A wingover placed my fighter back in the action fifty feet over the waters. Sure enough, there was a last bomber clearing the run and starting for home base. With a little motion of the rudder and stick I lined up the Wildcat for a head-on run, coming down on him from a little above his flight path. It didn't take long to bring the bomber fully within the rings of the projected gunsight on my windshield. I locked on fast and quickly let go a short, deadly burst of machine gun fire. The burst caught the left engine and smoked it as my tracers also hit and shattered the pilot greenhouse area.

As I flashed by the bomber and looked down into the cockpit, I clearly saw a third man, kneeling behind and between the two pilots, reach over and pull the pilot in the left seat (who was slumped over the controls) off the controls so that the copilot could take over. This was a flash view at high speed, but as any pilot will agree, motion in the cockpit or on the ground is readily seen, regardless of velocity. Motion in a cockpit and velocity are mutually exclusive. The motion of this third man was the factor that caught my eye. The pilots looked like mannequins at the controls. I could not confirm this aircraft as destroyed, so it went on the records as a probable kill. I wonder if they made it back to the airfield. I know many pilots said after the war that fighter pilots shoot down planes and not men. I could never accept this. Although I knew that I had killed men in the planes I shot down, it was either kill or be killed, and I felt no remorse for them. We were at war!

On Saturday, November 14, we were sitting around the pilots' Ready Room, waiting for a briefing when a patrol of ground Marines came to the tent and asked if there would be any enemy ships coming down the Slot tonight. This was a daily

ritual with these ground forces. We respected them highly.*
Word had come down from the coastwatchers that we could
expect such a shelling tonight.

By 0100 hours (1:00 AM), we were awakened by the Red Alert
signal, a banging on a metal shell casing hanging in the area. I
remember our skipper yelling, "Shelling! Hit the foxholes!"
Although I was half groggy from sleep, I was not the last man in
the foxhole. The hole was full of water and mosquitos. I became
really frightened as the 14- and 16-inch shells began to fall all
around us. My knees were shaking and I could not control them.
Others in the foxhole also experienced this. I suddenly realized
what war was all about. The Japanese were trying to kill us!**

*Even with reconnaissance aircraft available, the foot patrol was still the
best way to gather intelligence on enemy activity.

**The adverse environment also contributed to the list of casualties on
both sides. Malaria and diarrhea incapacitated many. And it was rainy and
muddy, endlessly so!

When John Keenan arrived on Guadalcanal in February-1943, he
described in his diary the rainy environment that was so familiar to all of us.
Read these excerpts.

[Sunday] 14th [February 1943]
At Cactus with the Cactus mud and slush.

[Monday] 15th [February 1943]
Cactus mud and slush again.

[Tuesday] 16th [February 1943]
Ditto.

[Wednesday] 17th [February 1943]
More mud.

[Thursday] 18th [February 1943]
Cactus and mud.

[Friday] 19th [February 1943]
Ditto.

During a lull in the heavy shelling needed to cool the guns, some of the pilots left the foxhole to look around. This played right into the enemy's hands as the destroyers opened up and continued the firing. There would be no letup since the ships fired alternately. It was only the next day that we were informed that battleships were also in the action. We knew that they could only shell a certain length of time and would have to leave in order to be out of the range of our fighters and bombers the next day.

These visits were called the "Tokyo Express."* However, unknown to us at the time, these were advance forces in another enemy attempt to regain control of Guadalcanal. The battle then in progress has come to be known as the Naval Battle of Guadalcanal. Like I mentioned before, this battle is well documented elsewhere. I shall not give an account of it here. The strafing of armed Japanese soldiers who got into lifeboats from their sinking troop transports is too horrendous to describe. But it was a simple fact. Kill them before they get ashore and kill you.

[Saturday] 20th [February 1943]
Ditto.

[Sunday] 21st [February 1943]
Ditto.

[Monday] 22nd [February 1943]
Condition Red again and I tell you I did not like it. More mud and slush. [Keenan, *op. cit.,* pp. 36-37].

*Along with these to and fro "rat" runs, there was another nightly annoyance dubbed "Washing Machine Charlie," one of several alternately-flying Japanese bombers (with their distinctive-sounding engines) which dropped impact-fused bombs. The bombs were sometimes dropped at the beginning of their run or during the middle of the run or at the end of the run as they began their return journey. This kept us in the foxholes, guessing and sleep-starved!

The engines were not synchronized. Each ran at a different pitch. The beat frequency of the propellers was the washing machine sound, which made it difficult to track. First though, "Louie the Louse" would illuminate the area with long-burning parachute flares. Men trembled during these nights, though the air was not cold! Although our 90mm antiaircraft guns vainly sought to down these planes, it finally dawned on us that three or four night fighters would have done the job. Unfortunately, none was yet available.

Chapter 13

Falling Brass

For the balance of November, flights were routine as the air action slowed. It was then that we lieutenants became aware of RHIP (Rank Has Its Privileges). We were scheduled for the dawn and dusk patrols where little or no action would be forthcoming, while the captains and majors had the noon flights—the action period.

During the early part of December, word came down from Fighter Command about how Japanese float planes were shooting down some of our dive bombers during their rendezvous after pullout. It was suggested that we change tactics when escorting them. After every four dive bombers made their bombing run, one fighter would dive down with them and be there for the rendezvous. It was a good idea.

Lieutenant Jim Percy, a truly top fighter pilot, had a big dogfight over Munda one day. His division of planes was sent on a fighter sweep to represent our squadron, VMF-112, and ran into a heavy overcast. Suddenly, a lone Zero appeared and made a run on all four Wildcats. Jim laughed at such a stupid move by a Japanese pilot, and figured, as his division took on the Zero, that the Japanese was not long for this world. To make a long story short, this Japanese pilot must have been one of their top aces. He made fools out of all four pilots.

Lieutenant Percy had the Zero in his gunsights and started firing when both planes disappeared in the clouds as they dived straight down. Soon the Zero came climbing out of the clouds like a homesick angel, heading straight up. On his tail and firing blindly came Percy. The tracers came through the cloud cover before Lieutenant Percy emerged. The Zero sped away. Percy's plane stalled and spun out at the top of his loop. We did not know that he had blacked out in the dive and was holding down on the trigger while semi-conscious. After he recovered from his spin, Jim's wingman pulled up, noticed that he was covered with blood, and assumed that the Japanese pilot had wounded him. Such was not the case. Lieutenant Percy had pulled too many G forces and blacked out while climbing after the Zero with such force that he struck his face on the gunsight. We did not have shoulder straps on these first tour planes. Regardless, Jim made it back to safety. We all had a good laugh about the top Japanese ace.

At high noon on December 18, I flew one of the fighters escorting a group of dive bombers scheduled to bomb the Japanese airfield at Munda on New Georgia Island. It was a beautiful day for an escort mission. Weaving over the slow-flying dive bombers, I became distracted and splashed around in my mind the awesome firepower of this little fighter. What destructive power for one man to handle! Why, only yesterday I was a college kid, roaming the campus and looking at all the beautiful girls. Now I was in this environment. What a change! The sound of conversation over the airways broke my daydreaming, and I focused on the situation developing rapidly before me. We were at the target area and the dive bombers were doing their thing.

After the first twelve had completed their run on Munda Field, I dived with the last four. Still in my dive, I spotted a float plane on the tail of one of our bombers. The Japanese plane was below and behind the tail and unseen by the rear gunner of the dive bomber. Both planes were heading directly into my line of flight and my gunsight. To save the lives of the pilot and his gunner, I would have to fire above his cockpit into the Japanese plane on his tail. I usually fired with four guns during combat and saved two guns to come home on as added insurance, but this time I switched on all six .50s. It would be a close, quick action. If I missed, the enemy pilot would shoot down our dive bomber. But I couldn't miss since his plane filled my gunsight and I had the proper lead on the gunsight rings. I surprised the Japanese pilot when I opened up. In his rush to make a sure kill, he had failed to see me coming until it was too late. I could see his frantic motion to maneuver out of my line of fire when he did spot me. I had put enough rounds in his plane before he could break clear of his position on our dive bomber's tail. The float plane went down.

In my anxiety to protect our bomber, I failed to realize that all the expended brass from the fired rounds were falling free of my aircraft below the wings. The Law of Free Falling Bodies would take over! With the same velocity as my fighter, the shell casings rained down on Lieutenant Poole's plane. The result was awful. It almost knocked them out of the sky, but luck was with them. They were not injured, but sore as hell. The plane would have to be repaired or scrapped. I completed a wingover and blew the damaged float plane out of the skies with a short burst from six guns.

It was then that Lieutenant Tom Hughes of VMF-112 joined

up on my wing for the return trip to Guadalcanal. He had witnessed the whole action. As we cleared the area, Tom's voice
came over the radio. He had spotted another Japanese float
plane returning from antisub patrol, heading right for us, but
a thousand feet below. The pilot saw us, and his rear gunner
began to swing his machine gun in our direction. I pulled into
a wingover and hopped down onto the tail of the float plane. I
didn't bother to dive below his plane and come up under him
for a firing position to avoid the rear gunner. I felt that firing
six .50s instead of the usual four would get him before that
peashooter could reach me. I was wrong. The rear gunner put
about five arrows into my fighter before I chopped him down.
I was closing too fast to stay on his tail and shoot the plane
down, and had to pull up quickly to avoid crashing into him.

At that moment, Tom Hughes boresighted the float plane
and opened fire. His firing was very accurate, striking the gas
tank and depth charges of the Japanese aircraft. I felt rather
than saw the explosion, and witnessed small pieces of plane fly
in clouds all around me as my fighter lurched upward with
tremendous force, as if seized by a giant hand and flung aloft.
By the time I straightened the fighter, Tom was on my wing
looking for damages to my aircraft. Finding none, he proceeded to move his hands in Hollywood film pantomime, taking my
picture and laughing. I did the same thing to him since this was
his first kill. We proceeded all the way back to Guadalcanal
doing these motions. Fortunately, there were no Zero fighters
around. It may appear that a fighter plane has an advantage
over a float plane. Such is not the case since the rear gunner
can shoot down the fighter. If the fighter plane overshoots the
float plane, there is the chance that the pilot of the float plane

may shoot down the fighter since no plane can outrun a bullet.

Upon landing, I was greeted by Lieutenant Poole. He was a little bit unhappy about the brass falling all over his plane, but was glad we all made it back okay. He said his gunner was going to nail the Japanese, but from my position I doubted that he had the angle to fire without doing damage to his tail. Regardless, he thanked me for my help. Lieutenant Poole was killed later during the war in an operational accident.

Chapter 14

A Beacon in the Night

That same evening we scrambled on a Red Alert call. It was drizzling and the weather was closing in rapidly. Four planes from VMF-112 were on standby and were airborne in short order from the cow pasture, Fighter One. I was the number two man in this division. We were told by radio that enemy planes were coming in under the weather front. By the time I finally got my wheels cranked up into the belly of the fighter, I had to hop on instruments.

It would be impossible to hold a division formation with the weather socking in so rapidly and night rising from the earth to engulf my fighter, so we were scattered in flight. To fly at 500 feet on instruments over an island with mountains can be sticky business. Nevertheless, I knew I had just cleared the island in a take-off to the east, so a left turn would put me over the ocean sound. I executed the turn with a standard two-needle width turn, holding at 500 feet until I was on a reciprocal heading of west.

Still on instruments and fighting rough weather, I decided to drop down under the overcast. I broke out at about 100 feet, and over water—thank goodness. Darkness was upon us and I wondered how the others were making out on the gauges. To compound the problem, I lost radio contact with Cactus control. Unknown to me at the time, two other fighters also lost contact. The last pilot had correctly read the closing weather and darkness and simply left his wheels extended and, flying at treetop level, circled around and landed.

For pilots right out of flight training and with little instrument time, flying off the waters at low altitude in darkness and turbulent weather is a situation not conducive to long life. By this time, I had guessed that Condition Red was false. Enemy planes would definitely be unable to strike our small piece of real estate. After half an hour of pure hell on and off instruments at very low altitude, I became apprehensive about my situation.

I flew a rectangular pattern (on instruments) over the waters and was on a westerly heading when I glanced back over my left shoulder and saw what I thought was a beam of light. My heart skipped a beat as I banked madly toward this source of light. There it was—beautiful. It was a beacon in the night. I zeroed in on this light source, like a moth to a flame, at an altitude of less than a hundred feet. We didn't have radio homing devices in our fighters.

Soon I reached the light and was happy to see the dark outline of Fighter One adjacent to this source. I was careful not to look directly at the light after having been on the gauges so long. I dropped my wheels and was making my approach, when it dawned on me that there were other fighters in the air. Since we all had our wing lights out for security reasons, a midair collision was a distinct possibility. I was committed in my landing pattern and sweated it out. I even braced myself for a possible crash into a fighter landing ahead of me. My fears proved groundless—I was the last plane to land and was the one Fighter Command was anxiously awaiting. This experience sharpened my wits. Never again will I take off in foul weather without making a decision for a possible quick return.

Now that I am on the ground and safe, I would like to share with the reader a short course on instrument flying. "Flying contact" means simply looking at the horizon and the earth below which is a point of reference needed to keep the plane flying level and on course. Let us change this situation. When a pilot's reference to the earth has been removed, at night or in clouds for example, his sense of balance will be confused and vertigo will set in. This is a feeling of not knowing whether the plane is diving, looping, upside down, or in an unusual position. In the pilot's mind, the plane is flying straight and level, which is not the case. Birds, when blindfolded, will flutter and drop to the ground. Hence, wise birds (and all are wise under these conditions) never fly when they cannot see. Only the "human bird" has been successful in doing this, and only with the aid of instruments.

A pilot cannot at one and the same time fly contact and fly on instruments. He must commit himself to one or the other. It is *mandatory* that he believe his instruments or he is as good as dead. Vertigo is such a strange feeling and is manifested in many ways. If a pilot, flying contact, enters a cloud with his aircraft in an unusual position, climbing and banking at the same time for instance, then he has a problem of orientation. He must immediately go on instruments. His mind tells him that his plane entered the clouds climbing and banking, since he lost sight of the earth at this point. He attempts to level his aircraft before flying an instrument pattern. When he has done so, his body remains conformed to the position of the craft as it entered the clouds. He is physically leaning to the right and back. His instruments tell him he is flying straight and level and he really is! But his middle ear remembers his last contact with the earth, climbing and banking. The pilot now straightens up and then his airplane takes on the position of climbing and turning. This unusual situation continues until the pilot shakes off the feeling. He must do this rapidly or crash. I would close my eyes, shake my head, and then look straight at the instrument panel. This corrected my vertigo every time.

The six basic instruments for blind flying are the artificial horizon, directional gyro, magnetic compass, needle and ball indicator, altimeter, and airspeed indicator. These instruments are still found in today's modern jet aircraft since they are fundamental and reliable for backup. However, with the advent of computers and complex radar and transponders, instrument flying is no longer "blind flying."

The bottom line of basic instruments is the needle, the ball, and the airspeed trio. These instruments are the ones on which every pilot (today's included) relies. The needle and ball indicator is a gyro type. The rudder controls the needle. Any slight turn to the right or left is noted immediately by the position of the needle. If the needle is centered and pointing straight up, the craft is not turning. If the needle is to the right of center, the plane is turning to the right. The ball located at the bottom of the needle is in a liquid cage between two wire lines. If the ball is centered then the aircraft is not banking right or left. If the ball rides the high wire to the left, the craft is in a left turn and if the ball rides the high wire to the right, the craft is in a right bank. If the ball is outside the cage, the plane is in a skid. The next gauge is the airspeed. Simply center the needle and ball, and then pull back the control stick if the speed is building up, and push forward the stick if the speed is slowing down. When the speed remains steady and the needle and ball are centered, the plane is flying straight and level. Then you take over and fly on instruments from this position.

Chapter 15

The Land Down Under

During the latter part of December 1942, I was waiting on the flight line for my plane assignment. Major Duke Davis had just returned from a wild dogfight and was landing the fighter I had been assigned. As he taxied back to the flight line and climbed out, he was swearing a blue streak and mumbled something about going back up and getting that Japanese. His chin and Mae West life jacket were covered with blood. The plane was riddled with bullets and a 20mm cannon shell had exploded in the cockpit with shrapnel clipping the major's chin. Needless to say, I was assigned another fighter.

Our first combat tour was over and we were scheduled for rest and recuperation in Sydney, Australia. To get there we had to fly back to New Caledonia, where we would hop a MATS plane bound for Sydney. The trip there was a delight. The sights over the Coral Sea were fantastic. The Great Barrier Reef, stretching for miles across the waters above Australia, appeared to be a huge crescent-shaped, emerald-green gem. What a sight!

We landed at Sydney Municipal Airport, a grass field reminding me of pictures from World War I. We were placed in busses and transported to the Australia Hotel in downtown Sydney. After room assignments, we went down to the bar for a few drinks and took to the streets. The Coathanger Bridge in Sydney was a refreshing sight along with Hyde Park and Bondi Beach complete with shark nets. We attended cricket matches and had steak and eggs with a liter of hops. We wondered what the "peasants" in the war zone were doing, since we were living here like kings.

The seasons in the Land Down Under are reversed. My hotel room was warm at this time of year and had a few mosquitoes. The seasons are the result of the fixed 23.5-degree tilt of the earth's axis. As the earth circles the sun, the northern hemisphere is closer to the sun for six months and the southern hemisphere for the other six months of the year. In the northern hemisphere, the spring (vernal) and autumn equinoxes mark the passage of the sun north and south of the celestial equator, respectively. But the northern hemisphere's spring equinox is the southern hemisphere's autumn equinox!

Also, the flora and fauna there are unique. Most notable in Australia are the marsupials (primitive mammalian animals) such as the kangaroo, koala, bandicoot, and wombat. Their newborns are nursed and carried in a pouch. Because Australia is isolated by an ocean, the marsupials were able to flourish to this day. Interestingly, the only marsupials to survive outside of Australia are possums and a small, insignificant group of similar animals located only in South America. Yes, their young are carried in a pouch! Possums were able to survive outside of Australia because of their tree-living habits. Actually the correct name is opossum. My association with this lowly, humble creature in Louisiana would later prove to be comforting and literally "lifesaving"!*

*A Southern culinary delicacy is possum baked with sweet potatoes! During the depression, resourceful young men made some money by selling killed and skinned wildlife. But many buyers would insist that one leg remain unskinned (on a rabbit, for instance) so they'd know they were not buying cat ("roof rabbit"). Some would kill and skin large field rats and pass them off as squirrels!

Finally, as all good things come to an end, we boarded the plane back to New Caledonia and the war zone. The pilots took turns flying. Lieutenant Lou Smunk from the Bronx gave us quite a scare over the Coral Sea some two hours into the flight. We were sleeping on the floor of the aircraft. He decided to awaken all of us, but instead of coming from the cockpit to do this, Lou simply cut off one of the engines. This brought the whole bunch of us forward and we didn't breathe until he started the engine again. Youth!

Later our squadron flew up to Espiritu Santo for regrouping and retraining. The fighter strip was hidden among coconut trees. The only outlet was toward the ocean. The runway was short, and there was a control tower at the top of a huge Kuani tree, a good seventy-five feet up. Among the new replacements was a pilot, Lieutenant Joe Lynch, who was to play within the next few days an important role in my life. His memory recall probably saved my life.

During this period, we lost another of our pilots in an operational accident. Lieutenant Cleveland was scheduled for a predawn take-off and was in the act of doing so when his fighter collided head on with a dive bomber taxiing down the middle of the runway. Both pilots and the gunner were killed, and .50-caliber bullets exploded in the fire that followed.

The next day we moved up to Guadalcanal. This was the month in which I would become an experienced and matured fighter pilot. I would survive three ordeals that convinced me Someone was looking after me. I realized many of us would be killed in combat, but I always figured it would be the other fellow. After this tour, I felt that I would survive the war.

Chapter 16

In the Wake of the U.S.S. *Jenkins*

On January 28, 1943, our squadron returned to Guadalcanal for the second six-week tour of combat. I would fly only three days on this tour. We flew fighters from Espiritu Santo to the 'Canal, a distance of a couple of hundred miles, and landed on Fighter Two airstrip. Something new had been added. Guadalcanal was coming of age. More planes were on Henderson Field and Fighter One. Now we were on a mushy, coral-filled pit with Marston matting for a runway and a take-off straight toward some tall coconut trees. These we could do without, but such are the hazards of war.

Predawn of Friday, January 29 was one for instrument flying. The moon was down and it was as black as the inside of a 1926 ink bottle. I was assigned a mission to fly this hop with three other pilots in a predawn take-off, vector east of Guadalcanal to 10,000 feet, and then orbit until daylight. Word had filtered down from Fighter Command that a Japanese force of Betty bombers would strike at dawn from the east. My plane was a clunker with a right wing tank attached.* It was dirty from mud splashes. After just clearing the trees on take-off, I sweated out the long climb on instruments. Movement from the bay below caught my eye as destroyers began to turn at high speed in the

*Our particular model of planes utilized only one wing tank placed on the right or left, but not both wings, because of a single fuel line. See the note in chapter 8.

water. This created huge phosphorescent waves as the propellers churned the ocean. It was a beautiful sight, preternaturally so. A hauntingly bright greenish-yellow hue, with an ambient, ghostly glow, lit up the entire bay.* It gave me a feeling of security as I relaxed, flying on instruments. I was oriented with the earth below. It was then that I noticed a film of oil rapidly spreading all over my canopy, and the oil pressure needle on the engine unit gauge dropping. Soon the oil pressure was zero and the engine began to seize. I was too busy to radio my troubles to base, or to the other fighters, as I dropped below into the blackest of nights.

I had just cleared 6,000 feet and was on the way down. My only sensible option was to bail out. Only a fool would ride down a fighter with a dead engine at night over water. I could no longer see the bay because the ships ceased to churn the waters below. I had trimmed the fighter to a speed of 130 knots and stepped out on the wing three different times as I held on to the canopy. Each time I lost my nerve and stepped back into the cockpit. I had had a flashback of one of our pilots bailing out during a dogfight and watching him go down pulling at his jacket in frantic gestures when his chute failed to open. Usually our chutes were repacked every thirty days,** but here in the

---

*Chemiluminescence, including bioluminescence (cold light, without heat), is the emission of light that accompanies certain chemical reactions such as the light emitted by a firefly, the above agitated marine microorganisms, or the oxidation of yellow phosphorus.

**Before it is deployed, a parachute is packed compactly so that air resistance is slight. When it opens, it moves away a larger amount of air as it comes down. This means more air resistance and slower motion. Someone coming down in an open parachute hits the ground with about the same speed he would have if jumping from a ten-foot height.

Heavy steel ships float on water because the overall density (total weight divided by total volume) is less than that of water, its interior being hollow. Long ago, the suggestion to build ships of iron was ridiculed because everyone knew that iron is heavier than water!

humid climate, the chutes were opened and repacked every fifteen days. My thoughts were wild. Did I have a chute that needed repacking? The one I wore was not my regular chute, so I elected to ride the fighter down on instruments. At night with no moon, it was suicide to try it.

Luckily for me, the air-raid alarm sounded and came over the radio to us. This started a chain reaction with the ships in the harbor below as they began to swerve and churn up the ocean with high-speed evasive movements. This provided me with a "landing field" complete with lights furnished by the sea-animal life acting like thousand-watt bulbs. The U.S.S. *Jenkins* steered a straight course for about 200 feet before turning. Here was my runway. I dropped the seat as low as I could get it and went on the gauges. As I approached 100 feet of altitude, I went on contact vision and dropped the little fighter wheels up in a most beautiful water landing. Seconds before I hit I remembered the wing tank I should have jettisoned, but this probably prevented my wings from dipping into the water for a possible cartwheel landing. The fighter simply skidded on the waters, nosed up past the ninety-degree-vertical plane, and bounced back below the vertical. This gave me time to get out of the craft before it sank. The tail disappeared below the surface as I popped my Mae West life jacket—called such because, when bilaterally inflated, it was reminiscent of the now-late popular actress.

The men aboard the *Jenkins* spotted me and yelled to pick me up on the run. This I refused to do. Any fighter pilot in his right mind will *never* board a destroyer during an air raid. I would take my chances in the water. I personally saw Japanese dive bombers sink one of our destroyers in seconds. Later they fished me out of the water and laughed at my fears about boarding a destroyer during an air raid. Visual (light) communications were established with Guadalcanal, and three hours later I was back with the squadron. Little did I know that I would bail out of my fighter two days later without the slightest hesitation.

The next day we lost another one of our NAP pilots. Staff Sergeant Conti's plane hit a chuck hole on take-off, losing flying speed. He could not clear the trees and crashed to his death. I took off over the crash site after Lieutenant Jack Maas.

Chapter 17

Winged Over Vella Gulf

The air war heated up around the Solomons and Fighter Command began to send strikes at maximum range against the Japanese. This finally put us on the offensive. All during the dark days of 1942 we had been fighting a defensive action over Henderson Field. Now the action was moving up the chain of islands. The range of the Wildcat fighter was about two hundred miles without external fuel tanks, provided the engine was functioning properly. As already mentioned,* the earlier Wildcats could have one wing tank attached for additional fuel. These external tanks were experimental and not too reliable in the hookup stage. However, emergencies in war have priority over safety, and the Wildcat was the only fighter we had to oppose the Japanese. The Corsair fighter would have had the range with its internal fuel tanks and efficient external tanks, but it was still a month away from the Solomon Islands campaign.

The coastwatchers on Vella La Vella sent word to Fighter Command that a Japanese fleet was seen entering the Kolombangara area between New Georgia and Vella La Vella, escorting cargo ships, and requested immediate dive-bombing action for a "sitting duck" attack. This sighting led our leaders to believe that another attempt to regain control of

*See note in previous chapter.

Guadalcanal was in the making, but the reverse was actually true. The Japanese planned to evacuate their troops from the 'Canal. The big fight was on Sunday, January 31, 1943, as twelve SBD-3 dive bombers, escorted by a handful of fighters (six Wildcats), were ordered to strike a fleet located 250 miles away from Guadalcanal. It would be one of my wildest dogfights and would earn me the Medal of Honor.

Eight pilots from VMF-112 were on standby alert for the afternoon action. We had been playing acey-deucy when word came down from above that an escort action was handed to Fighter Command. We scrambled for the flight line and, with parachutes strapped on, headed for the assigned Wildcat fighters. The briefing had been short and concise. The time was 1500 hours (3:00 PM), the distance 250 miles out, and there would be instrument conditions for the return trip since the moon was down and the weather was closing rapidly up the Slot. Wing tanks* were quickly attached on the eight Grumman fighters, and we were ready to go. Now the fighter action would be reversed. We would be fighting away from our field and over enemy waters with the added burden of a wing tank. Before engaging in combat, a fighter pilot had to jettison his wing tank for two reasons: the added weight hindered maneuvers, and if the external tank were hit by bullets, it would explode because it was not self-sealing.

I checked the new wristwatch that I had obtained in Sydney, Australia, designed especially for the "Bush Country." It had a leather cover over its face that could be lifted in order to check the time. I had removed my other watch from my wrist and placed it in my pants pocket, wondering how the new watch would stand the altitude test. I lost both watches in the coming action!

*In *Top Gun*, these wing tanks are erroneously referred to as belly tanks.

I was assigned a fighter that had a blond "bombshell" painted on the cowling with the title *Impatient Virgin* lettered underneath. The plane captain handed the yellow sheet to me for my
signature of acceptance and I signed. We made small talk as he
helped me strap in and said that he hoped I would get my first
kill this day. I mentioned that I already had a few planes to my
credit and this aircraft was not the one I usually flew. There was
a misconception after the war that all fighter pilots were issued
a personal fighter. Such was not the case. Planes were put into
commission on the flight line and then assigned at random.
Each plane did have a flight captain who was responsible for
seeing that the aircraft was in commission. I wish that I had
taken the time to remember his name, but I didn't. I regretted
losing his plane in the coming action.

The afternoon flight was not one of the more lucrative ones
and was usually shunned, if you could get out of it. But we were
on call and had no choice. It was after 1500 hours (3:00 PM) by
the time we were airborne, because the slower bombers had to
take off first. All eight of our fighters took off, and soon the
pilots switched to wing tanks in order to use all the petrol from
those tanks first, then release them to have a "clean" fighter
and lots of fuel remaining for the coming fight. Twenty minutes into the flight, one of the pilots called in with a rough
engine and aborted the mission. Two minutes later another
fighter pilot called over the radio, stating that his fuel-pressure
gauge was acting up. I wanted to tell him to smash the gauge
and not worry about it, since we needed all the guns we could
get on the escort mission, but I decided not to say anything. He
aborted and returned to base. That left six fighters to do the
job. I resented this a little since almost every fighter we flew
into combat had something wrong with it. If we were stateside

and in training, I venture to say that out of twenty planes we flew in combat, only two would meet flight standards. Some pilots were aggressive. Others were not.

Of the six fighter pilots remaining, all were members of VMF-112 (as were the two who had left), except Staff Sergeant Jim Feliton (a member of VMF-121). The VMF-112 pilots were Lieutenant Tom Hughes, Lieutenant Joe Lynch, Lieutenant Jack Maas, Lieutenant James Secrest, and me. It was decided that Maas and Hughes would fly high-cloud cover, and the rest of us would wing it right over the bombers for the dive on the Japanese fleet. It was never clear to me how this decision was reached, but the die was cast. After this decision we leaned the gas mixture as much as possible to conserve fuel. I had settled down to cruising speed, drawing fuel from the wing tank and scanning the area for enemy planes. We were now deep in enemy territory.

It was during this scanning action across the cockpit instrument panel and out the canopy that I noticed the gas-gauge needle starting to fluctuate. Fighter pilots are able to scan over the main instruments in the cockpit by simply looking across the panel briefly and watching for vibrating gauge needles. Movement of any gauge needle meant trouble. I quickly turned on the emergency fuel-pump switch and started working the wobble hand pump to build fuel pressure back to normal. The gas selector switch was on external tank, but the needle continued to drop in spite of my efforts. I quickly switched my selector valve to the main internal gasoline tank. The pressure needle jumped back to normal and my engine picked up added revolutions. I could not have used up the fifty gallons so soon, or had I? Either the tank had run dry from a gas-guzzling aircraft or suction was lost through the external connecting feed lines, the latter being a common occurrence in the experimental phases of auxiliary tank connections.

Quickly I got out the plotting board and did some fast figuring with the circular slide rule located in the lower-right quadrant. I could make it if I leaned out the fuel mixture some more. We were past the point of no return, and I could see the island of Kolombangara sliding past my wing 14,000 feet below. The Japanese airfield looked deserted. Where were the Zero fighters? We crossed the island and I checked my fuel gauge again. It was dropping rapidly despite my efforts to lean out the engine. I now knew that I had drawn a gas guzzler or had a main leak somewhere. I leaned out the fuel mixture until the engine began to drop RPMs. That was the signal to quit the procedure. It was going to be a close one getting back. I notified the others of my situation.

By this time we were over the target and the fleet below. All hell broke loose as the dive bombers went into action and the AA fire started reaching for us. Secrest and Lynch went into a strafing action against a cargo ship below, and Feliton and I were in position to protect the dive bombers against float-plane action. I picked up a call for assistance as the dive bombers came under attack while regrouping at 1,000 feet for the trip home. It had been a lousy run for them. All twelve had succeeded in getting near misses—no hits. I broke off my engagement and saw the usual old "Munda airfield" setup. That is, float planes were racing in to clobber the dive bombers after they started to join up. I was well experienced in this type of action and had the altitude advantage.

Two of the Japanese float planes were closing in for the kill, one following the other in a tail-chase pattern. With luck I could nail them both. I called for Staff Sergeant Feliton to follow me down and cover my tail in case I missed and overshot. In this way he could nail the float if I missed, and I would go after the next one. I had the feeling of perfect control as I pulled the little Grumman fighter flat on the trailing float plane for a no-deflection shot using only four guns. The rear gunner opened up on me, and I dropped quickly below his flight path to the six o'clock position and opened up with my guns when his plane filled my sights. It flamed immediately and dropped off in a slow graveyard spiral, burning furiously. The float plane exploded as I flew over and settled on the tail of the second one, the leader. Evidently there was no communication between this rear gunner and the pilot, since no evasive action was taken.

I settled onto his tail (below sight of the gunner) at six o'clock to him and twelve o'clock to me. When the aircraft filled my gunsight, and with the crosshair dead center on the cockpits, I opened fire and watched the plane flame immediately. The float plane started a slow climbing turn to the right from an easterly direction to a westerly one. Upon reaching the westerly heading, the plane exploded in a flash that matched the setting sun. For a moment I was mesmerized by the sun and this flash. It all seemed unreal. What appeared to be a slow-motion bit of action was only a matter of seconds. All other float planes cleared the area. I pulled up in a climbing right bank to verify Feliton's position and clear my tail. As I raced for altitude with Feliton on my wing, somebody over the radio yelled, "Zeros!"

About ten Zeros were heading straight for us and holding a fixed altitude. They failed to see Feliton and me, since we were about 500 feet below them in a climbing-attack approach. I pulled up into a smooth gunnery run on the leader, and it was like shooting at a fixed-target sleeve that I had fired upon during advanced cadet training. I placed the gunsight in line with the leader's flight path and a few mil-rings above the nose of his oncoming aircraft and squeezed the trigger when he was in range. There was no way to miss. The leader never knew what hit his plane or where the fire was coming from. With a jerking motion of such violence that it almost tore the wing off the Zero, he rolled out of my sights in a tumbling flip to the left. I either killed him instantly and his last reflexes resulted in this motion, or he was the fastest evader I had ever seen. I never saw him again and could not claim him. His wingman started upward in a slow left spiral climb, looking around and trying to figure out what was happening as I locked onto his tail. The Zero pilot started a slow roll upward and I followed the roll with him. As he came out of the roll, I fired. He never knew what hit him because his plane exploded violently.

This started one of the wildest dogfights I had ever been in. To this day, I cannot tell how many Zeros came down on us. Targets were everywhere. Staff Sergeant Feliton and I flew a defensive scissor weave covering each other's tail. On one turn, he pulled too wide and in the first few seconds, which seemed like a lifetime, I watched his fighter take a hit in the engine* as he banked across the nose of my fighter, leaving the fight with a huge trail of black smoke. The Zero broke off firing at him and cleared out when he saw my fighter. Staff Sergeant Feliton would be safe from further fighter action. Crippled aircraft were usually left alone in dogfights until all the action was over. Then they are shot down. By this time, Feliton would have bailed safely out. Although Jim Secrest was out of ammunition because he had strafed the ship,** he chased a Zero off my tail

*The Wildcat has an air-cooled radial engine.

**The Japanese ship Secrest and Lynch strafed caught fire internally and sank on a coral reef. Feliton and I also strafed the ship during this action. See chapter 29. Today, this sunken ship, the *Toa Maru*, is a museum piece for scuba diving, an added attraction for tourists visiting the Solomons.

during the dogfight by flying above my cockpit and attempting to crash the enemy plane. This probably saved my life.

For ten seconds the air was clear of fighters. My fighter had taken a few arrows during the dogfight, and I remembered seeing a Zero plunging in flames from above. It was a kill by Lieutenant Maas, who was up on high cover. The dive bombers had all assembled for the return trip and were preparing to take a heading back home. I noticed two Zeros closing in from behind me as I started a climb toward a position that would take me above the dive bombers, which already were fast disappearing in the distance. A glance at my fuel gauge shocked me. I had used up quite a bit of fuel during the dogfight.

The fighter escort mission was completed with the safe retirement of the dive bombers from the immediate combat area. If I stopped to engage Zeros, my chances of returning safely would be in question because I would probably run out of gas. With total darkness for the return trip, I kept thinking about the night water landing, something I did not want to consider again so soon. I decided to challenge the Zeros and take my chances, and at the same time draw them away from the dive bombers. If I ran out of fuel returning home after the fight, I would bail out this time. No more water landings on the gauges for me!

The coming action would be in full view of the rear gunners in the dive bombers returning to Guadalcanal and, unknown to me at this time, in full view of a missionary on the island of Vella La Vella. I would hear about this later. I switched on the last set of guns, the ones I usually kept for the return flight home, as added insurance. I have always maintained that if you can't hit them with four guns, you certainly won't hit them with six of them. But I was in an "all-or-nothing" position.

Those Japanese pilots were aggressive. Both fighters came at me as I turned head on into them. Again I was in the better firing position. A climbing head-on run is better than a diving head-on run. The Zero pilot had a trim problem diving on me as he picked up speed, while I was slowing down as I climbed toward him. I had six .50s against his two 7.7mm machine guns. I assumed my bullets would reach him before he could hit me. Besides, he couldn't use his slow, low-muzzle velocity cannons until he had me boresighted. My fighter became more stable as I slowed in the climb, and the Japanese pilot started shooting out of range. The tracers looked like Roman candles and a pair of railroad tracks coming at me. We closed in less than a heartbeat and I fired. The Zero caught fire immediately but kept coming straight at me. He was going to ram! The firing slowed my fighter about fifteen knots or more (*for every action, there is an equal and opposite reaction*—Newton's Third Law) and my controls became sluggish. This was intensely frightening! Could I maneuver out of the way? Frantically, I held the trigger down and the Zero blew up in a flash of fire. Pieces flew everywhere and some struck my fighter. I struggled to regain control from an almost stalled position after flying through the debris.

I banked sharply to get on the tail of the other Zero as he flashed by, but he had already pulled up high above me and completed his turn. He came in on me in a high-side run. Lieutenant Colonel Bauer always claimed that if ever a Zero gets on your tail, don't worry because he will open fire with the twin 7.7mm machine guns to line you up, then cease firing and open up with his twin 20mm slow-firing cannons. You will have plenty of time to skid out of the way. Even if they hit you, the armored plate behind you will take the shock. This man had convinced us long ago that the Zero was *not* invincible but could be dealt with head on or on your tail. He said, "Dogfight them, for they are paper kites." We knew from intelligence sources that if we were outmaneuvered by a Zero we could always go into a vertical dive at 200 knots, roll, and turn to the right. The Zero could not follow through for any gun lead on you because the Zero was not built for these stresses. So why not dogfight them? Our armor plate and bulletproof front glass gave us an added edge in head-on or tail deflection shots.

The Zero pilot coming down on me was too eager for the kill and did not judge my speed correctly. With his altitude advantage and his closing rate of speed too great and increasing during the diving run, he stood a good chance of overshooting me, a factor he realized too late. I chopped the throttle, skidded, and dropped my flaps. The Wildcat was down to a few knots above stalling speed. The Zero pilot, closing too fast, sailed by and overshot me, at the same time fishtailing his aircraft to stay on my tail. This he failed to do. I can still see his face as we locked eyes in that instant. He "froze" on the controls and flew straight ahead of me without making any attempt to get away. I shot him down with one short burst. It is odd how this action is still so clear in my mind today. I have often wondered if this Zero pilot knew that others were on my tail and, by flying straight, they would shoot me down after I got him.

I had made the near fatal error of not clearing my tail before I shot this Japanese pilot down. Unknown to me, there were others behind me, already in firing position and making a run on me. With a quick glance I looked at the watch strapped on the inside of my wrist and noticed the time approaching 1800 hours (6:00 PM). Night was rising fast from the earth below. (Night and lightning rise from the earth to the sky.) In the next instant I felt the watch fly off my wrist. The instrument panel erupted in flames caused by a 20mm shell that came over my left shoulder. The gasoline from the ruptured primer on the instrument panel had a good fire going in the cockpit, aided by the floor auxiliary fuel tank. In the next second I caught another burst in the engine. It flamed and lost power. In my frantic effort to get out of the line of fire I caught a glimpse of the Zero banking for another run on me. In the meantime the damaged canopy worked loose from its railings and, with a loud bang, was lost in the slipstream. With the aircraft falling apart, I unbuckled my safety belt and jumped for the trailing edge of the left wing. Feeling a jerk on my neck, I realized that I had forgotten to disconnect my throat mike cord.

How peaceful it felt to be free of noise and watching the waters far below as I tumbled through the air. What a sensational feeling! I felt free as a bird and got a beautiful view of the earth from "space." I had the feeling that I could land without getting hurt. I often wonder how others who have parachuted felt on the first jump. I don't remember pulling the rip cord (D-ring), but the next minute the canopy of silk (in those days, linen) was above me and I was slowly descending. My attacker had seen me shoot down his buddies. Through briefings, I knew that some Japanese pilots shot at Americans in parachutes, so I was anxious to get down. After bailing out of my stricken fighter, I had unfortunately reacted too quickly. Instead of free-falling at least 1,000 feet, clear of the dogfight arena, I found myself in the same sky with the Zeros! Helplessly exposed, I decided to play dead, just like the possums in Louisiana would do. I let myself go limp, with head sagging, as the Japanese pilot circled me twice. He even pulled his canopy back on the second pass and gave me the once over. I guess he fell for it, because he sped off back to Kahili Field on Bougainville Island. Or perhaps he was an honorable adversary.

The sun was setting as I floated down, and the waters below looked calm and glassy. I would not have to fight choppy waves but would have trouble judging when to release my chute before hitting the water. We were trained to let our feet touch the water before jumping out of the parachute harness in order to prevent the chute canopy from settling over your head and drowning you before you could clear the area. I concentrated on the glassy ocean below and had to wait an eternity, since I had left the fighter at about 2,000 feet. Finally I knew that I was close and said to myself, "What a piece of cake." I unstrapped my chute harness and sat comfortably in the seat pack, ready for my feet to touch the water. As usual, these instructions were for choppy waters, not glassy ones.

Depth perception over glassy water requires a great amount of concentration. If the waves below are choppy, the pilot will see 3-D immediately and will most probably judge the proper parachute height. A glassy ocean will not be readily judged in terms of height above the water. Compounding this factor in combat, a downed, wounded pilot would have more of a problem judging distance. This flashed through my mind as I was coming down, and I knew that with little wind the chute would collapse on top of me as I hit the water. Therefore, I would release about ten feet above the water and avoid this danger. Though I had excellent eyesight (20/10), I misjudged the distance, an understandable error after the fight I had just been in. What I thought was ten feet turned out to be over forty feet.

It seemed like an eternity before I hit the water while my chute collapsed and I fell clear of the shroud lines. My plunge into the ocean was a deep one. I was so far under that I had to pop my Mae West life jacket to help me reach the surface. I could see the reflection of the sunlight on the surface of the ocean, but it seemed like ages before I broke clear and gasped for air. Only half of my Mae West was inflated. The other half had been cut by shrapnel. The adrenalin was flowing and I didn't realize that I had been slightly wounded in the arms, leg, and side. My .45 automatic, canteen, and extra shells had been ripped off my waist when I bailed out. Had I worn my shoulder holster, which in my haste I had neglected to do, this would not have happened. By the same token, long exposure to the ocean's salt water would have rendered it useless anyway, quite likely irreparably. The backpack of my parachute harness still attached to my body contained survival equipment.

I had landed in the Vella Gulf between Kolombangara and Vella La Vella and beat Jack Kennedy to the island by six months. I started to swim toward the island of Kolombangara, hoping to get ashore and possibly steal a Zero from the Japanese airfield that I had spotted as we flew over earlier.* This

*See Louis L'Amour's short story, "Night Over the Solomons," published in 1943, in which the lead character reaches Kolombangara from a torpedoed ship. In a 1986 introduction, L'Amour notes the coincidence in that Jack Kennedy and I both reached Kolombangara from the sea. "Sometimes the imagination precedes reality," he writes. (Louis L'Amour, *Night Over the Solomons* [New York: Bantam Books, 1986], pp. 1-19.)

Navy Lieutenant (jg) John Fitzgerald Kennedy, who would become our nation's thirty-fifth president and the fourth to be assassinated in office, commanded *PT-109*, a patrol torpedo boat. In August, 1943, *PT-109* was split in two by a Japanese destroyer. Kennedy and some of his crewmates swam to Plum Pudding Island off the coast of Kolombangara. He was awarded the U.S. Navy and Marine Corps Medal for saving the lives of several of his crew. Plum Pudding Island was later named Kennedy Island in honor of JFK. I would meet President Kennedy at the White House seven months before his assassination.

See also the movie *Firefox,* starring Clint Eastwood. I first had the idea of stealing a plane! Conversely, in the coming battle for Iwo Jima, a Japanese pilot trying to infiltrate American lines was captured. He claimed that he was ordered to steal a B-29 bomber and fly it to Japan! He couldn't understand how that would help the situation on Iwo Jima but was willing to try anything.

may sound desperately farfetched, but I figured this was my best option, unless I elected to hide out for the duration of the Solomon action. Having been reared in the Louisiana swamps, I thought that I could survive in the jungle with no problem.

All aviators flying over water carried chlorine pills in their shirt pockets. These we were told to break in the water every fifteen minutes to ward off sharks. Sharks are vicious in the South Pacific, especially the great white ones. My wounds were not too bad, but bleeding filled the water and I feared sharks. I broke some chlorine pills every few minutes and let the smell permeate my flight clothing. But I found out after the war that they have no effect on sharks. The bombing may have scared off the sharks in this area, but that is only a guess.

The arriving darkness gave me a sense of security from the Japanese, and I hastened to swim. Swift currents kept sweeping me out to sea, and in my weakened condition, it took about six hours to reach shore. The darkened shoreline appeared menacing and the mangroves treacherous. Suddenly, a large fish brushed against my feet a few minutes before I reached shore. This gave me added strength to reach land. I was so tired by then that I simply pulled off the Mae West, hid it under the coral rocks, proceeded inland about fifteen feet, and, in a near state of collapse, I went to sleep on a pile of branches.

Chapter 18

A Life for a Sack of Rice

I awakened to raindrops pelting my aching body and noticed that my sleeping quarters were overhanging an entrenched gully. I had a breakfast of fresh water and a piece of concentrated chocolate from my survival kit, dressed my wounds from an emergency first-aid kit fit for a medical operating room, and headed east toward the far end of the island, toward a huge volcanic crater.

I remembered seeing the volcanic crater as we flew over the island. It was split into two halves and covered with jungle growth but rose 5,000 feet above the jungle floor. I was well oriented and felt that I could locate the Japanese base with no trouble while living off the land. Once I got within a few miles of the field, I would be able to hear aircraft engines and the usual airfield activities. I had absolutely no knowledge of any coastwatcher activities in this area. Munda Airfield, the Ghizo Island Japanese float-plane sea base, and Vila Field surrounded my position. I knew that I was deep in enemy territory and that the Japanese would be looking for me.

While I was moving toward the end of the island, a series of unlikely errors was acting in my favor. Sergeant Feliton was shot down before me. Our other four fighter pilots had returned to Guadalcanal, where Lieutenant Joe Lynch was debriefed in a

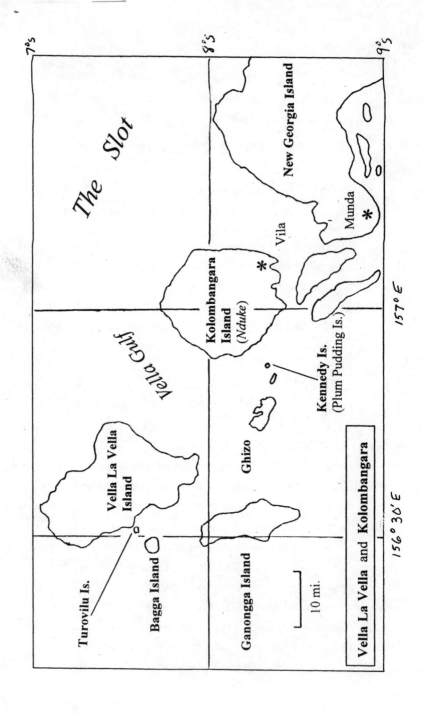

Vella La Vella and Kolombangara

session attended by Brigadier General Francis P. Mulcahy, who had replaced General Geiger as commander of Marine Air Wing One. Joe told the general that he had seen "a chute open up at a very low altitude above the trees of Kolombangara and collapse immediately among the trees." He marked the exact spot on his aerial-strip map and showed it to the general. Mulcahy instructed the intelligence officer to pass that information on to the coastwatchers. Joe had seen Feliton's chute over the island. Lieutenant Maas then reported that he had seen a chute open over the waters during the dogfight. That was actually my parachute.

The coastwatchers on Vella La Vella became aware of our downing. One of them, John Keenan, made a notation for February 1, 1943, in his diary: "Silvester's letters arrived telling us about our planes attacking the 2 D.D.'s [destroyers] and A.K. [cargo ship] yesterday afternoon. . . . Two messages . . . saying 2 fighter pilots shot down N. end of Duki [Kolombangara]."*

I am enough of a mathematician to know that the Law of Probabilities is not to be reckoned with. What would be my chances of fighting in the skies with Zeros over a great field of cloud actions, covering considerable distances, and being shot down over a spot in the ocean that enabled me to swim ashore, head through the jungle, and arrive at the exact place where Feliton's plane had crashed and his chute had snagged in the treetops? Remote, you will say. Absolutely not. Two days later I was camping below the tree where Feliton had landed.

When I realized that the jungle growth was too thick for me to make headway, I took to the trees. My wounds bothered me and I dressed them often, dropping the old dressings on the

*Keenan, *op. cit.*, pp. 32-33. Duki or *Nduke* is the native islander name for Kolombangara.

jungle floor below. I slept in the trees, in a "bed" between two huge limbs, on the second night. I didn't know what to expect on the jungle floor, because animal tracks were all around. Although I felt safe up in the trees, I also felt cornered. I painfully remembered how a possum would be hunted, often with the aid of dogs, and when treed would be shot or captured by means of a forked stick!

The next morning I spotted a clearing and dropped to the ground. I followed a trail through the jungle, holding my big survival-kit shark knife in full readiness until I reached coconut trees surrounding a clearing with a native grass hut in the center. The birds were singing as I listened carefully for signs of Japanese or other human life. I knew the sounds of the swamps of Louisiana well, and it's no different anywhere else. If the birds are singing, all is well.

The hut was neat and had a straw sleeping mat on the floor. Pretty soon I had a pile of coconuts and firewood, plus a supply of fresh water that I had obtained by brute force from huge leaves that acted like rain barrels. There were fishhooks and matches in my survival kit, and I would be careful not to leave any articles of civilization hanging around in case the Japanese crossed that way. A brackish stream ran through the compound and headed toward the sea, and I found native footprints on the banks. I wondered if they were friendly natives or headhunters.

After a repast of coconut milk and fruit, I decided to explore across the stream in the direction of Vila Field. Clearing the other side of the stream, I noticed that the tops of the jungle trees were chopped off in a neat path and realized that a plane had crashed. I hurried to the scene and twenty minutes later came across the remains of a Grumman fighter with the sound of flies all over the place. I searched in a radius of a few hundred yards but could find no body. During the search I found the remains of a chute—shroud lines and harness but no silk canopy. The canopy had been removed by someone. I searched for the .50-caliber wing guns, but all six were gone. I was paranoid about the Japanese, until I noticed native footprints all over the jungle floor. Later I found out that the coastwatchers had instructed the natives to retrieve the guns from downed planes. I salvaged what I could from the wreckage and returned to my hut.

I followed the stream to the ocean that afternoon and discovered an enchanting inlet with a beach across it. Crossing, I was waist deep in the water when I saw a huge shark fin cut the surface fifty yards away. I got back to shore just in time, losing one of my boondocker shoes in the process. The shark circled the spot where I had been for a few minutes, then went under. Shaking, I returned to the hut.

The absence of mosquitoes baffled me but was a blessing. Evidently certain vegetation was responsible for this. In the afternoon I heard the sounds of aircraft engines overhead and machine-gun fire. I found myself cheering from my makeshift hammock, saying, "Give 'em hell."* Later dusk provided me with an opportunity to bathe in the nearby stream and prepare for a good night's rest. What a life! I would be going to bed "with the chickens," as we say at home.

I awoke to the usual jungle noises and decided to make this a day of fishing. But by the time I had the lines prepared and was setting them in the stream, the rain was coming down in buckets. I returned to the hut. I didn't really know how to open

*John Keenan on Vella La Vella recorded in his diary a dogfight that occurred on the afternoon of February 2. See chapter 20.

a coconut and had been using the brute-force method with my shark knife. When I tried that again, I broke the blade's end off in a coconut and discarded it with the blade tip still embedded. Very hungry, I thought back to Louisiana down-home cooking, especially gumbo!

I awoke to a clear morning and listened for the usual jungle bird songs. The jungle was still. I grabbed my broken shark knife and looked out the hut door to see a short native standing at the edge of the clearing, looking at me. He had reddish hair in an Afro style and a bolo knife in his hand. I felt rather than saw the other natives behind me. There were six of them. I dropped my knife and they closed in to throw at my feet all of my discarded bandages, the tip of the shark knife, and the coconut itself, all the while grinning at me. They had been tracking me from the very first day. They touched my sunburned skin with one finger and marveled at the whiteness that appeared around redness, then one of them showed me how to open a coconut with a sharpened stick. I could see that I was out of my element in jungle ways, and I never forgot that lesson.

We had to communicate by signs. They moved me down a trail to the ocean until we came to a twelve-man outrigger canoe, then I was placed in the middle while they paddled near the shoreline for hours. We left the canoe in another inlet and followed a trail that led into a native village deep inside the dense overgrowth. There I was placed in a bamboo cage with two native guards outside. There were no women or children around. Past twilight, jungle drums rumbled, raising the hair on the nape of my neck. These drums were huge, twenty-foot hollow logs with a full-length narrow slit at the top. One native beat a tattoo code with two sticks and the women and children emerged from the jungle. They disappeared at dawn.* I was later told that they were hiding because they had been abused by the Japanese. The men and women were dressed only in loincloths, known as lavalavas. I was fed something that looked like spinach and fish. It was delicious. The women and children surrounded my cage and gave me the once over. I could see myself in the pot!**

The natives who had me in the cage were sitting around as if waiting for someone, and a group of seven new arrivals entered the village and began to converse with the group who had picked me up. Unknown to me at the time, the group's leader was Atitao Lodukolo ("Ati"—much more about him

---

*Years later, when I met John Keenan in Australia, he said that they kept me in the cage to prevent Japanese pilots from spotting a white man in the village. The penalty for helping a white man would be harsh on the village islanders, as the Japanese would strafe and bomb the village.

**The Solomon Islands' natives had very little contact with Americans or Europeans prior to World War II. They were not prepared for the great number of aircraft and battles in the skies above their land, let alone the material wealth they marveled at, such as canned foods, bottled drinks, radios, lamps, and weapons of war. To witness a white man descending in a parachute from the sky and coming into their midst was a cultural shock to them.

The economy of the islands depended to a large extent on copra (dried coconut meat yielding coconut oil), rice, timber, and commercial fishing. There was no national language. Pidgin English prevailed, with over forty dialects spoken among the different tribes found in the Solomon chain. In 1568, the Spaniard Alvaro de Mendana named the largest island in the chain Guadalcanal, after a town in Spain. Stories in those days about gold prompted him to name the chain of islands after King Solomon.

Headhunting continued into the twentieth century and was considered a way of life for the young warriors. I did not have any idea of what to expect from my captors. Although they showed signs of friendliness, their dispositions changed, unpredictably, from gaiety to moodiness. I tried not to betray my emotions while in their village. I found out years later that it was a custom to sacrifice human life by smiling at the captive and poking him for the purpose of obtaining a "last word." Upon hearing this word, the headhunter would kill his victim and name the next born child this last uttered word.

later). They threw down a ten-pound sack of rice and I was released from my cage to their custody. We quickly left the village without a word being spoken, but I knew that I had been bought for a sack of rice. This changed my whole outlook on life, and I realized how values of different cultures varied. The U.S. Navy would spend millions of dollars and use an entire fleet to rescue downed pilots, but this one had been purchased for a sack of rice. Very few people today know the extent of their wealth. I know *exactly* how much I am worth—a ten-pound sack of rice!

We took a break after about an hour, and the leader spoke to me in pidgin English. He talked about the coastwatchers, but not in those terms, and mentioned that he was sent to rescue me. I was overjoyed! I knew then that I would not be turned over to the Japanese. We entered another village and the chief wanted my belt buckle with the Marine emblem. Our intelligence officer had instructed us not to show fear when dealing with island natives or they would kill you. When he took my belt buckle, I grabbed his nine-foot spear in trade. It was a work of art, expertly and aerodynamically crafted, with a beautiful basket weave. The flying fox (tropical fruit bat) teeth and wing bones were sturdily mounted and lethally positioned on one end. It hangs in my den today.

We were told by the chief that a party of five Japanese was aboard a beached barge on a coral reef about fifty yards offshore. It was decided to get rid of them and make off with the goods aboard, since the Japanese had no idea that a native village was in the vicinity. The chief already had a Japanese cap. He gave it to me. Since I was a guest of the group, it was native protocol that I attend all functions, so I went along on the raiding party. We crossed a Japanese patrol (or were they the

Japanese who were aboard the barge and now leaving?) in the jungle but our group heard them coming before they heard us. When the leader signaled, we all "melted" into the tangled growth on each side of the trail, watching the noisy Japanese pass by. We could have easily taken them but our leader didn't want to betray our position and the coming action.

We reached the jungle clearing near the beached Japanese barge about two hours later. As far as I know, there weren't any Japanese aboard. Once inside, I looked around the radio cabin and found a bundle of papers that I brought back to Guadalcanal after my rescue. The natives took lots of clothing, guns, etc., and I searched a footlocker for clothing to replace my rags. I got a complete officer's summer khaki uniform, two pistols in holsters, a beautiful hari-kari knife in a gold and silver case, and a bottle of sake. I was feeling no pain when we left the ship. A picture of me in that uniform hangs today in my den. The uniform itself was discarded years after my return to the States.

I was anxious to leave the island of Kolombangara, and soon (could they sense my desire to get back to my lines?) a twelve-man outrigger was brought seemingly from out of nowhere. I thought that I knew the woods and jungles, but the way these fellows moved through the brush suddenly springing on you made me insecure, but happy to be on their side. A fresh crew of powerful young men from a nearby village did the paddling. We couldn't make the trip to Vella La Vella in one night because of the distance, so the journey would be in two steps. Between us was the island of Ghizo, with its huge float-plane base from which regular patrols were flown and native canoes were often strafed. The natives navigated in total darkness and in a rainstorm with no landmarks or stars to guide us. I tried to help with a paddle but

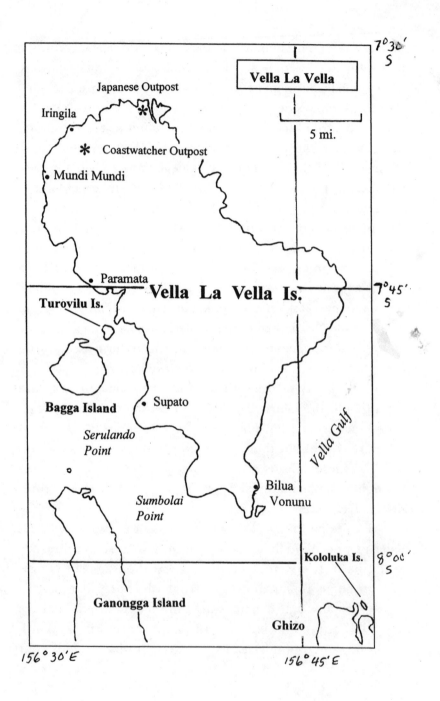

7°30' S

Vella La Vella

5 mi.

Japanese Outpost

Iringila

＊ Coastwatcher Outpost

• Mundi Mundi

• Paramata

Vella La Vella Is.

7°45' S

Turovilu Is.

Bagga Island

• Supato

Serulando Point

Sumbolai Point

• Bilua
Vononu

Vella Gulf

Kololuka Is.

8°00' S

Ganongga Island

Ghizo

156°30'E

156°45'E

only broke the natives' rhythm.* They let me know this when they took away my paddle and handed me a cup. So I settled down to bailing out the extra water while getting a good soaking from the downpour. We arrived at Ghizo Island before dawn.

The young natives left me with a guide and headed back to Kolombangara. We went bush all that day. At dusk, we followed a path that took us close beside a Japanese outpost. Wearing the Japanese outfit, I knew the penalties for being out of uniform in time of war (immediately shot or decapitated as a spy or slowly, horribly tortured!). Although I could see the Japanese in a squatting position eating around a campfire, we were not challenged. I could have sworn that one of the soldiers waved, but I didn't wave back. It was pitch black by the time we got to the other side of Ghizo Island, and I could hear the roar of float-plane engines. Maybe I could steal one and get back to base? But soberly I thought that even if I could pull it off, I would probably be shot down by one of my squadron mates.

---

*I found out years later that natives travel between islands by the "feel of cross-currents" through the bottom of the boat and that they correct their heading according to what they know is the correct vibration of the waves as viewed in daylight.

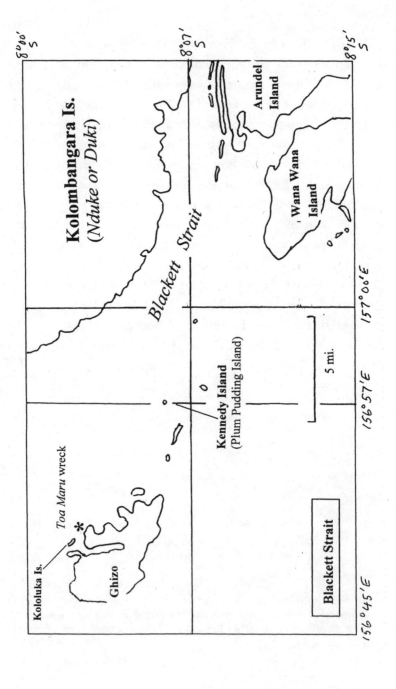

Kolombangara Is.
(*Nduke or Duki*)

Blackett Strait

Arundel Island

Wana Wana Island

Kennedy Island
(Plum Pudding Island)

5 mi.

Toa Maru wreck

Kololuka Is.

Ghizo

Blackett Strait

8°00' S

8°07' S

8°15' S

156°45'E

156°57'E

157°00'E

Chapter 19

The Lord Is My Shepherd

A fresh outrigger crew covered me with coconut palm leaves and would not let me up. This was a new ball game to me, and I had the feeling that this part of the trip would be more dangerous. I was right. We failed to reach Vella La Vella in darkness, and dawn found us an hour from our destination. Float planes buzzed us at daybreak, and the natives would stand up and wave every time one would pass fifty feet overhead. I had been placed dead center in the canoe and had visions of being strafed by float planes. The rhythm of the paddling and the drone of float planes made me apprehensive. Nervously, I tried to wiggle forward under the palms, but I immediately felt the end of a bolo knife on my chest. I got the message. Luck was with us and the rest of the trip was uneventful.

When the leaves were finally removed, I sat up in the canoe at a wharf adjacent to a huge, red, farm warehouse. I couldn't believe my eyes and ears when a white man and five native men appeared. Missionary Silvester called me by name with no errors in pronunciation. How could a perfect stranger in the middle of a war zone call me by name and rank? It was only later that I was able to comprehend the vast network of coastwatchers throughout the Solomon chain.

We walked up a slight grade to the living quarters and

compound of the mission. Missionary Silvester's home reflected the French culture of the region. His veranda had an excellent view of the air space above Munda Airfield on the horizon and Vella Gulf. We had tea at 1000 hours (10:00 AM) and again at 1500 hours (3:00 PM). I asked my host for a razor so that I could shave. He told me that a packet was being assembled for me and would be forthcoming. The things we take for granted in an affluent society take on a significance when you are isolated from these necessities. My quarters for the night were in the front room of his home, and I slept like a log.

In the morning (Sunday) I was presented with a toothbrush, a razor, and salt. After a good breakfast I felt great. I attended a beautiful Church of England service with the missionary after he told me that it would be an insult to the natives if I were not present, even though I am Catholic. I was amazed how heavenly they sang the hymns, and almost fell out of my seat when one native stood up and recited the Twenty-third Psalm, "The Lord is my Shepherd, etc." I had surrendered my weapons to Missionary Silvester, but had felt that the hari-kari knife was rightfully mine and kept it. I was wrong. He informed me very politely that I had a hidden dagger and the natives expected me to turn it in. There were smiles all around when I did so. Missionary Silvester told me that in exchange he would send me an ebony club after the war. I never received it.

That afternoon Silvester and I sat on his porch while our dive bombers struck Munda Airfield. We sipped tea at three as I watched the dive bombers join up for the return trip to Guadalcanal. Thereafter, the air was clear of fighters and float planes. I left for a coastwatcher outpost "somewhere in the mountains" within an hour, after being informed that a Japanese patrol was on the way to the mission. I thanked

Missionary Silvester for his hospitality, and also for the news that Staff Sergeant Feliton had preceded me and was in another village close to the coastwatchers.

I accompanied a party of eight natives as jungle drums relayed our progress along the way. The overland trip to the next village was dangerous. Because of my height over the natives, I would make an excellent target for snipers in the area, regardless of the Japanese uniform I wore. I found myself "shrinking" to blend with the moving party. I was also determined to hang on to the nine-foot native spear I treasured. After many hours and many silent fadings into the jungle growth along the trail to avoid the Japanese, we reached another village on the shore.* I found out later on that the place where I met the reverend was Bilua. The village we were now in was Paramata.

We found Feliton in Paramata. He was in bad shape and suffering from cracked ribs he had received during his descent. We didn't talk much because of his pain, but he was glad to be alive. We were both guests of the chief. A young woman, his daughter, fed us a tasty fish meal cooked in coconut oil. We were visited by one of the coastwatchers the next morning, namely, Lieutenant Henry Josselyn, a mining engineer from England who had been commissioned in place after the outbreak of war. This satisfied the terms of the Geneva Convention. The other coastwatcher was

*Thirty-three years later I found out that a New York Navy fighter pilot took this same route but failed to blend into the foliage when they ran into a Japanese patrol. Instead he panicked and dashed through the jungle growth, creating a definite directional noise pattern. He was cut down by concentrated fire from an automatic weapon shot in his direction.

Fifty-three years later, John Keenan let me know that had I not been picked up by Ati, a native islander, I would have been found by the Japanese who were searching for me. Evidently, the pilot who shot me down reported the parachute episode. Unknown to me at the time, the *Toa Maru*, which we strafed, was afire, another reason to look for downed American aviators.

a tall Australian officer named Lieutenant John Keenan. They made a good combination and were very effective. Since I was physically fit, Lieutenant Josselyn asked me to join them at the outpost and I quickly accepted.

We climbed for hours through the jungle before reaching the outpost. I described this post to Walter Lord for his book, *Lonely Vigil: Coastwatchers of the Solomons,* in which I am depicted, but he did not include the description in his text.* It was well planned for quick escape. The shelters holding the radio and other equipment were platforms over a deep ravine. They were secured by a stout rope tied to a common point overhead and ingeniously braced into a dragline configuration. All they had to do to strike camp and escape, after the radio was removed, was to sever the ropes with a single swish of a bolo knife. Everything would vanish into the deep ravine. The antenna wire for the forty-meter band could be removed in short order.

I am a C.W. (continuous wave radio) fiend and I told Josselyn that I could handle at high speed this part of the radio, but to my surprise, they used voice instead of Morse code to pass messages to Guadalcanal. Looking at the "slot" of islands in the Solomon chain, one could readily see that Japanese planes leaving Rabaul and Bougainville (Kahili Field) had to pass within sight of Vella La Vella, or they would run out of fuel on the return trip. There was no other way. A group of planes would be counted on the way out and counted again on the way back for the record. I saw the whole picture then! I had erroneously assumed that our radar was picking up these planes for advanced warning, but it was the coastwatchers all the time.

The next day I was fully indoctrinated on radio fix. The Japanese were restocking an outpost on the beach that we could

*Walter Lord also wrote *A Night to Remember,* about the sinking of the *Titanic.*

see at the base of our lookout. There were six Zeros flying cover for a Kawanishi flying boat. Three orbited at about 3,000 feet and three more were at 6,000 feet. Their orbits were clockwise for the first group and counterclockwise for the second. I could envision myself in a Wildcat fighter, diving at high speed from 20,000 feet through the formation of planes and burning the four-engined flying boat, a target I had been searching for a long time. They soon finished, and a destroyer pulled into the bay with a four-engined flying boat in the air above the island. We knew the planes would be coming down and that they were in position to get a fix on our station when we opened up. Sure enough, a flight appeared. We counted them and transmitted "25 planes heading yours" before shutting down the transmission. It was not enough time for a fix, so with amusement I watched the Japanese soldiers running out of the outpost below with fixed bayonets, looking like the Keystone Kops. They didn't know where to go or what to do and soon settled down. The Japanese destroyer quickly left.

I later heard a rumor that both Josselyn and Keenan were betrayed by the natives and killed by the Japanese, but Walter Lord told me in 1975 that this was not true. Josselyn was cool under stress. One day he was pursued by a Japanese patrol, but since it was 1500 hours (3:00 PM), he stopped to make tea, Japanese or no Japanese. He got away with it. I was to have tea with Lieutenant Josselyn at his home in England thirty-three years later, almost to the day. In June of 1944, Henry Josselyn and John Keenan each received the British Distinguished Service Cross.*

Soon it was time for Feliton and me to leave the island. The

---

*Keenan, *op. cit.*, p. 47. Keenan's citation reads, "For great daring and enterprise, for service in the Pacific Area." See also Eric Feldt, *The Coast Watchers* (Melbourne: Oxford University Press, 1946), p. 388. Josselyn received also the Silver Star for his part in guiding the first wave of U.S. troops to Guadalcanal on August 7, 1942.

rescue mission was scheduled for the afternoon of February 12, three days before my twenty-second birthday. I was eager to get away from the hazardous life the coastwatchers led, so I joined Feliton on the beach to wait for the arrival of an escorted P-boat. Under the very noses of the Japanese outpost and within sight of three enemy airfields, I saw for the first time our new gull-winged fighters, along with Army P-38s, flying escort for the P-boat. We were already in a canoe, paddled by Ati and another, having bid farewell to our benefactors, when the flying boat landed. I was ushered in, spear and all, with Feliton and Keenan. Dr. W. W. Evans, known to us as "Big D," was along for the ride. I said, "My gosh, Doc, you can be killed coming up here!" He laughed and handed me a bottle of brandy for medicinal purposes. Erroneous information had filtered down that I was seriously wounded. He braved this flight to help, receiving a medal for this mission. I will always be grateful to him. On the flight back one of the P-38 pilots had an engine run wild near Munda Airfield and the pilot had to bail out over the ocean. We surreptitiously landed to pick him up. This was a necessary ordeal, as we had to land on the open ocean within sight of Japanese-held Munda Field. Any slight miscalculation of wind drift would place all of us at the mercy of the Japanese. Only after we picked up the P-38 pilot and were airborne did we begin to relax.

The F4U-1 Corsair birdcage (called such because of the unique cockpit canopy) had at long last reached the front lines. I had the "distinction" of being rescued on the first mission that any Corsair pilots flew in the war zone, a rescue mission to pick up Lieutenant Jeff DeBlanc and Staff Sergeant Jim Feliton. Ken Walsh* was one of those Corsair pilots. He was soon awarded the Medal of Honor for fighter action.

*Lt. Col. Ken Walsh died on July 30, 1998.

Chapter 20

Selections from
John Keenan's Diary

John Keenan, one of the coastwatchers who rescued me, kept a diary during his service on Vella La Vella. Reprinted here are sections of the diary that give Keenan's account of our action and rescue as well as a flavor of the type of life the coastwatchers led. It was a harrowing life as can be seen from the following excerpt from the prologue written by John's wife, Phyllis.

The modest account presented by the diary of John Keenan and Henry Josselyn does not fully reveal the dangers and difficulties encountered. The reader has to imagine the dense jungle and proximity of the enemy, the chance of betrayal by pro-Japanese natives, mosquito-borne tropical fevers, tropical sores and ulcers, the continuous damp conditions, uncertain food supplies, lack of medical attention and debility produced by the prolonged heat and humidity. Added to this were difficulties with the cumbersome 3BZ radios, which were designed for a fixed location and not the portability to which they were subjected.

Walking tracks were often washed out and the dense jungle terrain, with clinging vines and plants with hooks and barbs, made it difficult to negotiate quietly in the dark. Living undetected, observing but unobserved on a small, enemy-held tropical island was a hazardous and lonely task for these intrepid men.

At this stage of the war it was by no means certain that the

U.S., Australian and New Zealand forces would gain dominance in the area. The Coast Watchers were in a position of extreme danger and vulnerability, in the heart of enemy territory.*

These are the meanings of some abbreviations you will encounter in reading Keenan's diary. D.S.I.O. means Deputy Supervising Intelligence Officer, who was stationed on Guadalcanal. The call letters used in radio transmissions by the coastwatchers are: DEL for the coastwatchers on Choiseul Island, PWD for the ones on Rendova Island, HUG (or KEN) for those on Guadalcanal, and NRY for Josselyn and Keenan on Vella La Vella. *Duki* is, as we have seen, the native islanders' name for Kolombangara Island. Here are the selections from John Keenan's diary.**

[Sunday] 31st [January 1943]
Rather a quiet day. 2 D.D. [destroyers] and an A.K. [cargo ship] went to Vila*** at 1530 and 9 transport planes bound for Vila at 1730 otherwise only activity a few isolated planes. A couple of B.I7-P.38 skulking about from time to time. Bamboo reported that they have a Nip. prisoner, one that was picked up on the 28th and as far as they can ascertain he is off a

*Keenan, *op. cit.,* pp. 3-4. The diary begins on October 14, 1942. The first entry (October 14) begins in Henry Josselyn's handwriting, but changes to John Keenan's handwriting. The remaining entries from October 15, 1942, through February 28, 1943, were all written by Keenan.

For many years, the diary lay forgotten in the family deed box. It was redis- covered in August of 1996. After John's death (April 11, 1997), his son Adrian and granddaughters Rachael and Tessa transcribed the diary. It was proofread by John's wife, Phyllis, and edited and formatted by John's younger son, Clive. The original manuscript is now in the Australian War Memorial, Canberra.

**Ibid., pp. 32-36. Reprinted with permission of Phyllis Keenan.

***Vila was the Japanese base on Kolombangara Island.

warship. Notified Mac and answer came!!! Tried to solder up the shower today to get it into working order. Had our Christmas dinner tonight—a plum pudding sent by Sir Phillip Mitchell. It was good too. The scouts arrived back from Vila late last night. Reported about the raids on Munda and Vila the last few nights. Apparently they have been pretty solid and have done quite a lot of damage. The airfield also has come in for some pretty big raids. Our set and organisation now function well. We have some of the lads well trained now as scouts and they do very good work. Worthy of mention is IKera trip to Segi and back Daniel and Ingapela's work at Vila. Silas is a wonderful help to us still and is really the backbone of the Vella natives. The only crew not pulling their weight well at the moment is the Supato village. Have kept wonderfully well to date. Josselyn has had a few off days. Now with a bag of rice* the boys found near Vila and the Jap chow we are also pretty well off for food. D.C.H. [Dick Horton] reported natives rumors that Japs have landed at Biloa??

[Monday] 1st [February 1943]
Rather a hectic morning. A few isolated planes before breakfast then after that 14 planes went N.W. and later returned S.E.—whose? Twenty-two and possibly more sighted out to the S.W. bound S.E. Apparently another Nip raid on Guadalcanal. Could not get through until nearly 1000 owing to conditions. Silvester's letters arrived telling us about our planes attacking the 2 D.D.'s [destroyers] and A.K. [cargo ship] yesterday afternoon. Later a ring from D.S.I.O. thanking us and D.E.L. for good reports and said attack successfully carried out. Wonder if they sunk the three of them. Two messages

*Was I traded for a sack of rice stolen from the Japanese?

from D.S.I.O. saying *2 fighter pilots shot down N. end of Duki** and a B.17 shot down over Munda Pt. After all this hectic a.m. was just about to make arrangements to go to Vonunu and Josselyn went out to the Observation Post to spot some planes and 20 D.D's [destroyers] buzzed off on E.S.E. course. Shot an immediate [message] off and HUG gave me two that D.E.L. has sent. They reported that same were C.A. or C.L. Then more planes and kept busy for most of the p.m. PWD picked up the ships at 1700 and sent off a frantic [message]. Eventually had some tea and left for the beach at 1745. On the way round to Paramata had to hide from a couple of low flying aircraft. Silas later told me they were both U.S. but did not take the risk. Eventually reached the boat at 2130 and got under way. Picked up Joe Martin at Supato and had a good trip to Vonunu arriving at 0145.

[Tuesday] 2nd [February 1943]

Did not know what was to greet me at Vonunu so went in very cautiously. *Silvester told me he had had a very low flying Jap. around his place all day.*** The A.K. [cargo ship] that was hit on the 31st was drifting with the tide in [V]ella Gulf, well down by the bows. This morning no sign of it but boys reckon they can see the mast behind one of the islands. Should be verification sometime this evening. Took down the telephones and the boys getting the wire. They look to be in good order. Silvester gone to Talito for the day. Spent most of the day getting down the telephone lines and the cups. There is quite a bit of it and it should act well at the Observation Post. Natives picked up a mast behind an island off Gizo-KololoKai and we think it may be the A.K. [cargo ship]. Late afternoon sounds of a dog fight to the S.W. but could not

*Emphasis mine.
**Emphasis mine. Was this Japanese pilot looking for Feliton and me?

see a great deal. Silvester arrived back at dark. Joe Martin and crowd left at 2000 from Gizo and went to bed feeling very tired. About midnight woke up to be told that there was a fire at KololoKai Is. Apparently is the boat and now burning well.

[Wednesday] 3rd [February 1943]

Had not been long back in bed when Arti* arrived back. A canoe had just arrived from Vavanga and had brought in the U.S. pilot Feliton who had been shot down over Duki. Got him up to the house and in bed and sent a letter off to Josselyn at 0530. I spent most of the morning getting him bathed and fixed up. After being shot down he landed safely by parachute, but got caught up in a high tree. Managed to get halfway down but got stuck and had to jump the rest—nearly 40' [feet]. In doing so dislocated his shoulder, hurt his ribs and is very badly bruised. However appears much easier and rested a little during the day.

Sam arrived late p.m. and went down to examine the launch. The 1st bearing gone—that is why there was so much noise coming down. Sam going to run a new one and he is getting the Chinese carpenter to put in a new stern. Should fix things well.

[Thursday] 4th [February 1943]

Feliton had a fairly good night. Letter from Josselyn written 1610/3(rd) to say no reply. Another written 2030/3(rd) to say try and get Feliton to Paramata before tomorrow afternoon. Will have to think things out a little. Sent word off to Banatoma for the big canoe. By the time it arrived and everything was arranged it was after 1200 when we made a start. Sam wrote to a Chinese carpenter at Falito to ask him to fix up the stern. If he will do so, will get the stern and bearing fixed together when we pull the boat up.

*Atitao Lodukolo. He is also known as "Ati."

Left Vonunu. After a good trip arrived at Paramata at 1830. I got well and truly cooked by the sun. Feliton had a good journey and did not appear to suffer a great deal. As soon as he went to bed he was asleep and slept through until after 1100. Letter from Josselyn saying arrangements had been made and that message would be sent off as soon as we arrived. A lot of aircraft up and down but fortunately for us was over to the East. It is a trip I would not care to do again by daylight. Apparently another naval engagement flared up south of Guadalcanal. No definite news yet.

[Friday] 5th [February 1943]

Feliton spent a good night and had some eggs and tea for breakfast. I hope the PBY arrives before lunch. I spent a night on the boards and it was not at all comfortable. Spent a very quiet afternoon. Had a haircut and feel much better. News from Josselyn saying pick up delayed and will notify time later. Hope they do not postpone i[t] for too long as Feliton requires medical attention soon. Letter from Silvester saying a little trouble down at Vonunu and would like one of us to go down immediately. Set out at 2100, leaving Silas and Abel to look after Feliton and instructed them to put him on the plane as soon as it arrives.

[Saturday] 6th [February 1943]

Had a very pleasant trip, feeling dog tired and slept quite a lot of the way. Arrived at Vonunu at 0430 and went straight to sleep. At 0600 Arti arrived with De Blanc, whom he found on the E. coast of Duki. Well but lacked clothes and shoes. Suffering a little from lack of food. Also some salvaged gear from the A.K. [cargo ship] came across. The A.K. [cargo ship]* slipped off the reef into deep water on Thursday morning.

*The *Toa Maru.*

Blankets, sheets, towels, rifle, ammunition, pots, clothes, papers and 5 bicycles among the salvage. Spent a very quiet day and was hoping to visit Lepo, pack up the salvage and return to Paramata but Kera says the launch not running well enough so will have to alter things. Anyway both De Blanc and Self need a good rest so we will sleep on it.

[Sunday] 7th [February 1943]

Awaiting news from Supato. Spent a very quiet morning. Heard a few bombs dropped on Vila. The Japs carried a Union Jack, Belgium flag, Portuguese merchant flag and a British colony flag on the ship. News arrived back from Supato that the PBY had not been yet so decided to leave that night by canoe and leave the launch at Vonunu. Boys have made arrangements to take several canoes across to Gizo-Gepo tonight and bring back some of the gear. After a wonderful lunch and dinner left at 2000 and had a good trip. Picked up another canoe at Supato. While crossing between Sevlanda Pt and Supato a distinct odour of oil and F. B. told us that she had found oil on the beach. Wonder what it was?? Brought back a rifle, ammo, revolver, flags—a few odds and ends. When Silvester has seen all the other he will send it along.

[Monday] 8th [February 1943]

Arrived at Paramata at 0430. Feliton very glad to see DeBlanc. Feliton much better and able to sit up a little. I doubt if his shoulder is dislocated, but it certainly is very badly bruised and torn. Ribs and stomach much better too and he is eating well. *Silas* gave us eggs, fish, fresh fruit etc and we did ourselves well.*

*Emphasis mine. Mrs. Tozaka, the fifteen-year-old daughter of Chief Silas, fed us.

I left De Blanc and Feliton at Paramata and made my way to the camp, arrived just before dark. No news yet of the PBY and the two lads may be with us for some little time. If so they may come up here in a day or two.

[Tuesday] 9th [February 1943]

Had a wonderful nights sleep and got up very late. Raining heavily. Quite a lot of lads have been shot down during the last two weeks all over the Broadway. Some been found and now awaiting a pick up. Looking through the book Josselyn has certainly had a busy time since I left and has had to keep going. Hope we have not to be split up again when so busy. Cleaning things up a little around the camp. A quiet afternoon:—no ships. The Jap rifle and revolver function O.K. so now we are not too badly off for firearms. Shot a bullock this afternoon so have a little fresh meat.

[Wednesday] 10th [February 1943]

A wet miserable day with visibility at zero. Heard a few planes about. Josselyn went down to the beach to see the lads. The thing Feliton and De Blanc cannot understand [is] how we live so well here. Much better than the boys at Cactus do. Fresh eggs, fresh fish, vegetables, fresh meat, milk, cream, fruit in almost unlimited quantities. The only thing we are really short of is butter, jam, flour, salt, etc. Seneki went out to try and salvage a Jap float plane that had been forced down off Gizo, but unfortunately there were two occupants and they later repaired the plane and took off. Went through the papers off the "Toa Maru" 9,180 tons and all ready to sent them to H.A.M.* Josselyn and De Blanc arrived back at 1800 and we had a good

*H.A.M. = H. A. Mackenzie, who was on Guadalcanal.

old confab and knocked over a bottle of Jap. beer—was it good. Good news from Russia* and good news that the Japs have evacuated the Solomons-Guadalcanal.

[Thursday] 11th [February 1943]

Had a good nights rest and stood the early morning watch. A couple of isolated planes skulking about but could not get the messages off till after 0900. Message from H.A.M. to say that Guadalcanal area was now entirely in Allied hands—great news. Also that the PBY will be along Saturday A.M. bringing stores, new assistant Firth** and that I have to proceed to Lunga for further instructions. It came with a burst. No activity all morning. The inventory arrived from Silvester and Josselyn will be able to begin a Quarter-Master and Ordinance store. Very quiet day. A further message arrived at 1815 saying that the pick up will be tomorrow afternoon. Had our farewell dinner—fish, fresh meat, beans out of our own garden, plum pudding, custard and even burnt the brandy [over the pudding]. Finished up with a bottle of Nip wine which was excellent, Luckies [cigarettes] and black coffee. What more could we wish for.

[Friday] 12th [February 1943]

Packing up and sorting out my gear. A few aircraft about and a Mavis sat down at Irringila for about 30 minutes. I wonder what it was doing. Josselyn was busy letter writing. Got away at 1100 and reached Paramata. The PBY (amphibious aircraft)

*The German Sixth Army was decisively defeated in the epic Battle of Stalingrad, which ended in early February 1943 with the surrender of Field Marshal Friedrich von Paulus.

**Sub-lieutenant Robert Firth replaced Keenan, who was ordered to go to Guadalcanal with Feliton and me.

arrived at 1600, escorted by F.4.U.* Took about 15 minutes to unload and off again. A P.40 came down off Munda and had to stop and pick him (the pilot) up.** Not very nice position (in the open sea) to be in for a pick up—However did the trick and took off without being molested. Arrived at Cactus at 1900 and took quite a while to get off the boat. General Mulcahy (?) met De Blanc and took us both around with him. Had a good iced whiskey and it was good, a good supper. Met a lot of the lads U.S. of higher rank but they seemed to give a solitary coast-watcher a good welcome.***

---

*Twenty-four Corsairs (F4U-ls) arrived on Fighter Two field, Guadalcanal, around 1400 hours (2:00 PM) on the afternoon of Friday, February 12, 1943. Twelve of those pilots were instructed to remain in the cockpits of their planes while their Corsairs were refueled. Those twelve formed the high-priority escort mission described by John in this diary entry. The Corsairs had the range for the round trip to Vella La Vella.

**Actually it was a P-38 as P-40's did not have the range to fly round trip for this rescue mission.

***I must bring into sharp focus here my doubts about John Keenan's survival. After my 1975 visit with Henry Josselyn in England, I had assumed that John Keenan was betrayed by the natives on Bougainville Island and killed there.

Jack Read, a coastwatcher, had organized a new network to cover the whole of Bougainville. John Keenan took over the northern coast with his base near the village of Lumsis. From his native contacts, Keenan realized that his position near Lumsis was in danger. Hiding his radio and barely escaping into the bush, Keenan narrowly escaped capture and probable death at the hands of the Japanese. The coastwatchers abandoned the island.

But Keenan and other coastwatchers returned to Bougainville in late October 1943 to prepare for Operation *Cherryblossom,* the American landings there that began on November 1. This is where I lost contact and I assumed that John Keenan had been killed. It was only when I attended the 50th anniversary (1992) on Guadalcanal that I received word from Martin Clemens, the top coastwatcher, that Keenan was alive and living in Brisbane. Five years later, I visited him in Australia.

Chapter 21

Advent of the Corsair

When we landed at Guadalcanal, I was transported to General Mulcahy's headquarters for debriefing. Dr. White (De Blanc in French), a Navy physician, gave me a physical examination. After debriefing, I was offered a position on the General Staff. One does not turn down a general's wishes. If you are a regular officer, it's bad for your career. However, since I was a reserve officer, I thanked the general and told him that I was already employed by VMF-112 and wished to get back at the Japanese pilot who shot me down. He laughed, turned to his staff, and said, "How about that!"* He released me from his offer.

One of the colonels on his staff asked me if I wished to fly one of the Wildcats to the rear zone with the rest of my squadron. I knew that this was a "test" thrown at me. It is axiomatic in aviation, after an airplane "accident," to get the pilot back into the air as quickly as possible or ground him, depending on his reactions. I quickly turned down the offer to fly a Wildcat back, but I confidently stated my desire to fly a Corsair back without even the benefit of a checkout. I added that the little Wildcat had let me down twice in three days, first an engine failure at night, then a gas-guzzling, "short range"

*I kept in touch with General Mulcahy over the years. He passed away in December 1973.

123

fighter. With my luck, I would probably have to land in the water or bail out on the 450-mile flight to the rear area. He laughed and let me take the transport back.

Our squadron left the combat zone for Espiritu Santo for transition to the Corsair. During the early part of March, a few of us elected to check out in the Duck, an amphibious plane. I was among this group and soon was an instructor for the others. The trick is to keep the stick all the way back on landing and hold it back, or else the plane will porpoise on the waters, which could be disastrous.

We visited the various islands and brought a 35mm projector with film and a generator to an island having a school run by nuns, for native boys and girls. It was a pleasure to see the children's faces light up when the movie screen showed New York City and other points of interest in the United States. But the icing on the cake came when fishing scenes were shown. They could identify with this and there were many oohs and aahs during these episodes. We left the equipment there. One of the Sisters gave me a letter for Betty Tatum at 8 Accord Bondi Beach, Sydney, Australia.

Before we checked out in the Corsair, I had the opportunity to visit the ground troops stationed nearby. I asked the C.O. if there were any Marines from Louisiana. I was soon reunited with two of my high-school friends, Dan Duchamp and his brother, Marcel. In a short time I had them over and had the pleasure of flying them around the island in our utility aircraft, the SNJ.

Most pilots went aboard the various ships in the harbor to scrounge ice cream, cake, and anything else not tied down. On one of these trips, I encountered another friend, Lieutenant (jg) Lamar Beyt, a dental officer, who was from New Iberia, Louisiana. He gave me a tour of the ship and I left with extra goodies. It was a refreshing visit for me. Later on after the war, we met again on the tennis courts. He is an avid tennis player and so am I.

The transition from the Wildcat to the Corsair was rewarding. The Wildcat was a good fighter. I found it to be the better platform for gunnery. It also had immediate and total forward visibility since it was primarily a carrier plane. But the Wildcat was vicious and unforgiving if you hit the brakes after landing. It would groundloop from burnt-out brakes and, with the landing field between rows of coconut trees, this often resulted in a change of engine. The cause of most of these groundloops in this aircraft was the pilot's false interpretation of direction as it touched the ground. Upon landing, the left oleo strut (hydraulic leveler intrinsic to carrier planes) would usually go down, causing the left wing to drop below the horizontal, which made the pilot believe the plane was swerving to the left. The normal reaction would be to apply the right brake. But if it was held too long, brake failure would result, hence, a groundloop. To land the Wildcat, the pilot must keep his toes off the brake pedals and use the rudder and elevators until all lift is gone. Then he must gently touch the brakes as needed to correct the path of the aircraft if it alters its straight landing course. This can be attributed to the narrow landing gear that was made for carriers, not for runways.

The Corsair, on the other hand, had a wide landing gear, which made for a more stable landing. But the price to be paid for this added feature was a loss of forward visibility on take-off. This was due to the high angle of the fuselage. You had to properly align the flight path of the craft with the runway or you would end up in the trees. The Corsair had a propeller about thirteen and a half feet in diameter and gull wings to support the craft and keep the blades from touching the ground.

This was the aircraft flown by Gregory "Pappy" Boyington and the Black Sheep Squadron.* Pappy came to the islands in the latter part of 1942 and joined us on Espiritu Santo for the checkout in the Corsair. During this training period, Pappy had his leg broken by one of the pilots of VMF-122. He was acting C.O. of this squadron and during a drinking session at the Officers' Club, his challenge to wrestle was accepted by one of the pilots, Lieutenant Shifflett, who happened to be a national intercollegiate wrestling champ! While they rolled on the floor of the club and out the door, we heard a snap and Pappy was on his way for medical treatment in Australia. In July before he took over the Black Sheep Squadron, Pappy became Commanding Officer of our old squadron, VMF-112.

I enjoyed the power of the Corsair and went through the usual high-altitude workout required for this phase. It was routine and I enjoyed Pascal's Principle of Hydraulics** used to

*Colonel Gregory Boyington, U.S.M.C., Retired, wrote *Baa Baa Black Sheep*, which inspired the mid-1970s weekly television show. In an interview with *TV Guide*, Pappy said that the series was very entertaining. His chief criticism, he went on to say, was that each week beautiful women of all nationalities would socialize with the main characters. In reality, he said, they wouldn't see women for months at a time! Pappy is now deceased.

**The Principle of Hydraulics refers to an increase in pressure at any point in a confined liquid, producing an equal increase in pressure at every other point in the liquid. For instance, visualize a closed liquid system with a small and large piston on each end. When pressure is mechanically applied to the small piston, this same amount of pressure then acts on every part of the inside surface of the system, including the large piston. If the area of the larger piston is, say, 100 times that of the smaller one, the total force on the larger one will be 100 times whatever force is applied to the smaller piston.

retract the wheels upon take-off. What a cinch! Press a button, pull a lever, and the wheels would retract. The same principle was used for the flaps. Beautiful! No longer would we have bruised shins from a slipped ratchet as the gear crank in the Wildcat swiftly unwound against your leg. I learned quickly to land with 30 degrees of flap instead of 50. At 50 degrees of flap the controls of the Corsair become sluggish and uncomfortable to the touch. When the wheels touched, I would raise the flaps to destroy all lift and the Corsair would roll out, picking up a few knots of added speed. This was the price to pay for a really good landing. At other times I would elect to land on the front wheels and slowly let the Corsair settle into the three-point position as it lost flying speed and lift. I always felt very comfortable landing the F4U-1, familiarly known to us as the *Bird Cage*.

One odd feature of this Corsair was its lack of a cockpit floor. The pilot placed his feet on runners, but below was a dark, empty well. If we flew upside down and held that position, trash from below would fall on us! We used to joke about being hit by a tool left by some mechanic. Later models had a floor.

During this transition phase, we lost one of our top fighter pilots, Lieutenant Wayne Laird. Wayne was a good friend of mine. We first met at ACTG North Island, San Diego. Like me, he was an amateur radio operator, so we had an interest in the radios used aboard Naval aircraft. While we were acquiring additional hours flying the Corsair, Laird decided to go up to 35,000 feet and try out the new VHP radio channels. He called in to us that he was switching frequencies for a check at higher altitudes. This was the last we heard from him. We searched the area for days and waited for word from the natives on the surrounding islands but were unable to confirm his demise. Could it have been anoxia caused by lack of oxygen at high altitude?

It was never established one way or the other. Shortly thereafter we moved back into the war zone. Our last tour of fighter duty in the Solomons had arrived. It was during this interim that I made sure that I got to know PFCs Bertaux, Bowers, Dejoy, Farnham, Fox, Hynde, and Kaszar, our Aviation Armorers.

A most damaging blow to the Japanese came in mid-April with the death of Admiral Isoroku Yamamoto, commander-in-chief of the Japanese combined fleet. He was the one who devised the plan for the attack on Pearl Harbor. All the while, he apparently believed that Japan lacked the means to fight a long war, saying that, with the Pearl Harbor bombing, Japan had awakened a sleeping giant. But as others have asserted, it would be more accurate to say that Japan had *disturbed a waking giant!*

Yamamoto planned to visit the island of Bougainville in the northern Solomons on an inspection and morale-building tour. Messages informing the local commanders of Yamamoto's impending arrival were intercepted by American listeners, promptly decoded, and passed on to the proper authorities.

Briefings were held to plan a fatal rendezvous, as Yamamoto had a reputation for punctuality. The Corsair was being considered for the job. But because of Bougainville's extreme range from Henderson Field, it was decided that the Army would be given the job. Their planes had the longest range. The attackers struck at 0930 hours (9:30 AM) on April 18, just as Yamamoto's plane began to land on Bougainville and as his own fighter escort turned to leave. Eighteen Lockheed P-38 Lightnings swooped down on the two bombers carrying the admiral and his staff. Brushing aside the remaining enemy fighters, they quickly struck down their targets. Yamamoto died, a victim of able intelligence work and skillful timing.*

On May 3 VMF-112 returned to the war. We now had a fighter that would match and surpass the Zero. All of the Japanese targets in the Solomons were now within the range and capability of the Corsair. On May 5 we received word of the placement of field guns in native villages on Kolombangara and the resupplying of the enemy outpost on Vella La Vella. Since I knew these locations from my previous experiences, I was scheduled to make the flight. We had 500-pound bombs strapped onto our Corsairs and a generous amount of machine-gun ammunition. Eight of us were scheduled to go on this fighter sweep.

The face of Guadalcanal had lifted. No longer were we taking off on muddy cow pastures. There were steel mats and a splendid control tower. It was like having in the war zone a stateside commercial airfield! What a far cry from our first tour of duty during the dark days. (Guadalcanal was secured on February 9, 1943.) We got airborne quickly and were on our way to the objective far northwest of Guadalcanal. As the island of Kolombangara formed on the horizon, I became more alert and a little uneasy. I quickly identified the spot where I had gone down. As we crossed the huge volcanic crater on the island, I saw the targeted village and spotted the objective among the huts. This was the very place where I spent the night and where I was exchanged for a bag of rice. I was reluctant to dive down on the village as I had a vested interest there. Torn by duty and loyalty, I elected to make the last run on the target

*Saburo Sakai, one of Japan's greatest aces, was partially blinded during combat over Guadalcanal on August 7, 1942. Suffering from severe head wounds, Sakai flew his damaged Zero across 600 miles of ocean to return to base! Years later, at a joint convention of American and Japanese wartime aces in San Diego, California, I met him. Saburo Sakai died on September 22, 2000.

in order to assess the damage. The destruction was awful. When I swung over for the dive-bombing run, I just could not release on target, but made sure my bomb fell into the surf shoal adjacent to the island and village. This brought a yell over the radio about such a lousy drop. Well, I am not a dive-bomber pilot.

The next target was a different ball game. I led the flight to the Japanese post near Paramata village on Vella La Vella. We all had aerial strip photo maps marking the spot so as to avoid any errors. I had the pleasure of making the first firing pass. I could even pick out our coastwatchers' position, but was careful not to betray it as I peeled off for my attack run. I could visualize Henry Josselyn and Keenan* watching as I flashed by at 300 knots and opened up with all six .50s. I watched my tracers converge on the Japanese outpost and saw the soldiers diving for cover. After many passes we broke off the engagement and rendezvoused for the return trip. Incidentally a flight of Army P-38s provided high cover for us. On all missions, high-cover fighters protect those engaged in low-altitude targets. With this action finished, I very much wanted to buzz the place where Josselyn was located, but I dared not betray his position by such a stupid move. Josselyn and I talked about this day thirty-three years later over tea at his home in England. His wife, Pat, had cakes and more tea for us as we mulled over old times.

There were many scrambles after May 10, but all turned out to be routine. Guadalcanal was becoming civilized. More troops were entering the area. We had fighter squadrons running out of our ears. Word filtered from the States on pilot training that reflected a Superman syllabus. Potential Navy and

---

*Although John Keenan had returned to Guadalcanal with Feliton and me, I did not realize at the time that he was leaving Vella La Vella for good. Only later did I find out about his reassignment to Bougainville.

Marine pilots were not sent overseas unless they had 500 hours of flight time and a course in jungle survival. I have always maintained that a will to survive is enough for survival, but such is not doctrine. I guess I shall always be a Reserve Marine.

On May 11 I received news from home that Alton DeBlanc, a first cousin of mine who was also in the Marines, was in our area. I found out he was a first lieutenant, stationed on the Russell Islands in the Solomon chain. I grabbed a Corsair and flew over to visit him. It was a joyous reunion. He asked me to slow roll over the field after take-off and I did. A visit such as this was one of the fringe benefits pilots receive. Another is even better. Whenever pilots are aboard carriers nearing the continental United States, many choose simply to fly to the West Coast ahead of the rest of the task force and have everything ready for the troops when they arrive. One covered many miles as a pilot and received a more composite picture of the war action. However, the ground troops did the hard fighting. Fighting in the air is a momentary thing, fast and furious, whereas on the ground it is a twenty-four-hour thing.

On a dark May morning I was assigned a predawn flight and taxied out to the service runway. I did not take time to line up properly with the runway lights. I just poured the coal to the fighter. When the tail lifted, I found myself headed straight for a line of parked fighters. As I had full throttle, I popped full flaps (50 degrees) and cleared the fighters by inches, almost in a stalled position, until I gathered enough forward speed to raise my flaps in increments of 10 degrees. Once cleared of the area and trees, I raised the last 10 degrees of flaps and I was in business. The fighter was heading for the heavens at flank speed. I barely got away with this one, but I would not have done so were I in the Wildcat. But of course, in the Wildcat, I would have seen the runway easily simply by looking straight ahead. So ended my last tour in the Solomons.

VMF-112 was a squadron with a unique group of fighter pilots. Two of our pilots survived during this last tour of duty there against million-to-one odds. Lieutenant Jim (Gilbert) Percy had his elevator controls and wing tanks shot out during a dogfight on June 7. Fortunately, his plane didn't explode. He bailed out at 2,000 feet with the craft propelling at a velocity of 350 knots. The chute, failing to open fully, trailed behind him. Striking the water feet first, he fractured his pelvis, sprained both ankles, and had 20mm wounds in his arms and legs. He was picked up by friendly natives and lived to return to active duty a year later.

The other VMF-112 pilot, Lieutenant Sam Logan, was also in this same dogfight on June 7 and was shot down as he went to the rescue of a P-40 pilot. He bailed out of his burning Corsair at 20,000 feet. A Japanese pilot made repeated firing runs on Logan. When he failed to hit him in the swinging parachute, he decided to ram him with the propeller. On the third pass he succeeded in chopping off part of Sam's right foot and heel, but a New Zealand pilot drove off the Zero before he could make another pass. Sam was picked up by a J2F Duck flown by Lieutenant Colonel Nathaniel Clifford. Sam too returned to flight duty after a year.

Our squadron VMF-112 would remain in the Solomons as a number, but with new personnel assigned to carry it forward.

Chapter 22

Training Other Pilots

We shipped back stateside aboard a freighter going eight to ten knots. It behooves one to think of the luxury we enjoyed coming over as compared to the trip back. All of the pilots remaining from our first tour would be aboard ship. Out of a complement of twenty-four pilots, two had been killed in action, three killed operationally, and three surveyed out for wounds. This isn't a bad record for having fought in Wildcats during the dark days of Guadalcanal, though the losses were regrettable.

Gone was the desire to solve celestial navigational problems and note the celestial stars. Instead we were usually on deck taking in added sun and eating better food, hoping to regain the weight lost in combat. The mental strain always in the back of our minds concerned U-boats and torpedoes. Only after we had crossed the International Date Line and the equator did we begin to relax and look at night for Polaris (the North Star). How well did we remember when this star slipped below the waves on our trip over in 1942.

Once again, I gazed at the canopy of stars, seemingly eternal and expanding into infinity. I pondered man's place on this planet, a mere speck in the immense cosmos.*

*Charles Lindbergh may have felt the same. He said, "After my death, the molecules of my being will return to the earth and the sky. I am of the stars!" Also, the older physicist in me has another point of view. There is no space

The approach to the United States had the added "fringe benefit" of swells created by waves striking the continental shelf, the slow rise and deep fall into troughs that can play havoc with one's stomach. Most aviators are immune to the effects of these swells. We gathered on the deck to place bets on the exact time the bridge of the ship would pass under the Golden Gate. A pool of cash was put in a hat and we were all assigned hour and minute numbers. The winner, of course, would buy the first round of drinks at the Top of the Mark in Frisco. Lieutenant Sam Richards won the bet and we anxiously awaited docking.

We pulled into San Francisco Bay. After unloading, we had one hell of a blast that night at the Top of the Mark, a bar on top of the Mark Hopkins Hotel on Nob Hill, overlooking San Francisco Bay. (The hotel and bar, still there today, opened in 1929.) Late the next morning we headed on our separate ways home. Further orders would be sent to us individually during our leave. I boarded the train for San Diego, made a P.X. run, and went to Lindbergh Field, where I took the noon flight for New Orleans. I slept the whole way.

It was good to be back with the family. My mother and father kept me eating good old Cajun food. I dated my high-school sweetheart, Louise Berard. Unknown to me, but known to Louise, the town of St. Martinville was going to honor me with a public gathering on the steps of the post office. The Marine Corps had sent an account of my exploits to my hometown newspaper, *The Weekly Messenger.** That afternoon, the mayor and town council had a planned presentation and I was brought

---

beyond the universe. Otherwise, it would be, by definition, part of it. The universe expands by actually "creating" new space between groups of galaxies. The universe is getting larger and the galaxies farther apart.

*Today, the *Teche News*.

in at the last minute. After the usual protocol, I was called on to speak. I struggled through an *ad lib* speech. Mayor Leo Buillard presented me with a new aviator's chronometer watch to replace the one I lost in combat—I had mentioned this in a letter to my parents. Many of the merchants in town chipped in for the price of this unique watch. It was an aviator's dream, a watch with character. I thanked the people who came. I sincerely appreciated seeing the good people of St. Martinville again, but I didn't deserve all of this. Others in different theatres of operations were doing their duty, which I felt certain was more than my efforts. Regardless I will always treasure this moment. Louise and I enjoyed an outing that evening with friends. Many were servicemen from St. Martinville with their wives.

Halfway through my leave, I received orders to report for assignment as advanced combat fighter instructor at El Toro Marine Air Base. This was in keeping with the policy of the Marine Corps and other branches of the service to use combat personnel as instructors, giving others the benefit of their experiences in the combat zone. Unlike in foreign nations, our pilots didn't continue to fight day in and day out until they were killed or survived to the end. A case in point was Captain Joe Foss. He was taken out of combat after he shot down his twenty-sixth enemy plane, tying the record held by Captain Eddie Rickenbacker of World War I fame. He was told by the generals not to come back to the war zone until he trained 500 other Joe Fosses. Jug Herlihy, a friend of mine who was in a dive-bombing squadron overseas, decided to join us as a fighter pilot. We welcomed his contributions to the training program. Our students were not cadets but commissioned officers just out of flight school. Each combat pilot was assigned eight student pilots for a syllabus of gunnery and fighter tactics. This proved to be a chore for me.

Without an automobile, I would not be free to hit the beaches of California. We were all captains by now. Secrest, my friend from VMF-112, had a brother, Howard, in Alexandria, Virginia, who knew someone who wanted to sell a convertible. This type of automobile was a must for all fighter pilots as it was a status symbol. I contacted him and sent $900, the price for the 1941 Chevrolet convertible. A recently married second lieutenant received orders from Washington, D.C., to El Toro. He drove my car across the country.

By January, I was bored with this duty and wanted to get back to a fighter squadron. On January 15, 1944, Lieutenant Colonel Paul Fontana, our former skipper from VMF-112 and an ace fighter pilot, wanted pilots for Ferry Command duty. Jug Herlihy and a few of us jumped at the offer. I had this extra duty until January 31, a red-letter day in my life, the anniversary of my being shot down.

We were soon ferrying to the East Coast old Grumman fighters for cadet training and flying back to the West Coast new Corsairs. This was excellent duty for me as it gave me the chance to stop off in Louisiana and visit my family and Louise. On one occasion, while flying an advanced trainer (SNJ-3) from New Orleans to Houston, I flew over St. Martinville and buzzed the law office of James Martin, where Louise worked as a legal secretary! On hearing the loud noise, Attorney Jim Martin exclaimed, "Who is that @!# fool?!"

On March 25, 1944, Captain Jug Herlihy and I were assigned to VMF-461, commanded by Major William R. Lear. Major Jack C. Scott was his executive officer. Major Elkin S. Dew would take over from August 21 to November 3, 1944. It was during this return to a fighter squadron that many combat veterans were assigned as a core group to help whip up the new young lieutenants into a fighting unit. I was placed into the squadron as the flight officer, the number-three man in the chain of command.

When Major Dew took over the squadron, he was a stickler for protocol and the lineal list of ranking officers. He called me in one day and said that Jug Herlihy had a higher number on the lineal list than I. Even though we had become cadets at the same time, he had taken his flight training at Pensacola. Jug's class was 10B-4 IP (P for Pensacola) and my class was 10B-41C (C for Corpus Christi). *10B-41* translates into the tenth month (October) of 1941, with the letter *B* standing for the second half of the month. (*10A-41* would be the first half of October 1941.) As Pensacola was considered the "Annapolis of the Air" followed in rank by Corpus Christi and Jacksonville,* Major Dew said that Jug should be the flight officer of the squadron. Rank has its privileges! Jug refused the position since I had made the first combat tour as a fighter pilot whereas he made his as a dive-bomber pilot. It didn't really matter to me one way or the other. It was my first encounter with service protocol. I knew then and there that the military would not be my career.

The efficiency of the flight clerks in our squadron was excellent and all I had to do was shuffle around papers and sign things prepared for me in advance between flight schedules. These men knew more about squadron procedures than all of us did. Our job was to fly and fight.

Most of us were up in age now (twenty-three years old) and the pilots we were getting for the squadron ranged from twenty to twenty-six years of age. Our squadron now held a complement of twenty-four pilots in six divisions, four planes to a division, two

*Pensacola, Corpus Christi, and Jacksonville were the Navy's only three advanced aviation training centers.

to a section. We trained in *finger-four* formation. If you look at the tips of the fingers on your right hand, omitting the thumb, this would be the formation we flew. The index finger is a wingman, the middle or longest finger is the flight leader, the ring finger is the section leader, and the smallest or last finger is a wingman. All four fighters made up the division, which was now the combat formation for all striking forces. This enabled us to have a better vision of all areas in the sky. It was much superior to the three-plane formation of World War I.

VMF-461 was based in El Centrē in California's Imperial Valley. This is a desert resort town and a bird sanctuary near the Mexican border and the Salton Sea. Truck farming was done late in the afternoon and far into the night and early morning. Desert heat discouraged activities between 1000 hours (10:00 AM) and 1500 hours (3:00 PM).

The squadron had F4U-1D Corsairs with the bubble canopy. It was an improvement over the *Bird Cage* F4U-1 we had flown in combat. The nucleus of combat fighter pilots included Captain Bill Baldwin,* Captain George "Jug" Herlīhy, Lieutenant Bill Kopas (our C.O. Exec.), and me. This training period gave us the opportunity to build up flight time and check out in all types of aircraft.

While I was there, my brother, Lieutenant Frank DeBlanc, U.S.N.R., flew to the West Coast in a commercial plane to visit me. He was on leave from his tour of duty in the Atlantic and decided to see how the Navy fared on the West Coast. It was a happy reunion as we hadn't seen each other since his enlistment. The relaxed atmosphere of the Officers' Club at El Centro

*Captain Bill Baldwin married the actress Kirn Hunter. During the forthcoming Okinawa campaign, Bill wore knitted pink booties strapped to the goggles on his helmet in celebration of the birth of his daughter. Today, his daughter is a judge in New York.

Marine Air Station was an excellent site to compare notes.

When the United States entered the war, Frank's cadet class from Jacksonville was earmarked for PBY-4s.* He flew patrol float planes for a while, then was given the PB4Y-4 (a four-engined plane, B-24 type) to fly the South Atlantic antisubmarine patrol from the Azores to Buenos Aires, Argentina. Because the Azores were off the coast of Portugal, Frank and his crew would fly into Lisbon for R and R. Most of his missions were routine with a minimum of ten hours in the cockpit for each flight. But there was one incident of terror. Off the coast of Portugal one night, he and his crew picked up on his radar scope a sighting that looked like a German warship. The moon was down, so the attack would have to be at high speed right off the waters, dropping the depth charges and bombs at mast height. Frank decided to risk turning on his forward floodlights to identify the target before dropping his load of ordnance. This flash decision saved the lives of a friendly ship that had strayed into unfriendly waters.

Because of Frank's outstanding performance on instrument flying, the Navy pulled him from the South Atlantic Patrol against German submarines. He flew the PB4Y-4 during hurricane season to get information on these storms. After the Atlantic hurricane season, he was back in the combat zone, chasing submarines.

*Frank went through his Navy career with ease and became a command Navy pilot, holding the rank of Lieutenant Commander U.S.N.R. This would have placed him in an excellent position to become an airline pilot after the war, but he opted to become a brother in the Maryknoll Order. He went to South Korea, just after the end of the Korean War, and spent over thirty years in the missions there. His sixtieth birthday was the occasion of *Hwang-gap*, a Korean rite of passage to the world of elders. Later, too ill to return to his beloved Korea, Frank died on January 25, 1999, and is buried at Maryknoll Center, Maryknoll, New York. [2000 note]

He was soon on his way back to Norfolk, Virginia, for reassignment. Rather than let him go to Los Angeles to catch his return flight, which went through Tucson, I placed him in the back seat of a dive bomber (SBD-3) and flew him to Tucson. Nearing Tucson at an altitude of 10,000 feet, I decided to barrel roll the dive bomber. Unknown to me, Frank had unbuckled his seatbelt and shoulder straps for comfort and was enjoying the ride with the cockpit hatch open. The roll was done and recovered very quickly. There was no danger of Frank's falling clear of the plane because a barrel roll keeps you glued to the seat with G forces. It's the same maneuver as taking a bucket of water and quickly passing it in a circular motion over your head. The water will not spill out. Contemporarily, it's like children defyingly extending their arms as a roller coaster loops. Of course, Frank wore a parachute. Had I done a slow roll, he would have had to hold on, yell into the mike for me to stop the maneuver, or pull the rip cord as he fell free of the craft. We had a laugh about this. We arrived in ample time for his flight. I even picked up a passenger for the return flight to El Centre, an Army Sergeant Baker. This was June 28, 1944, as shown in my log book.*

We practiced carrier landings on a large scale. I guessed that we were scheduled to go aboard one of the carriers for our next tour. Unknown to us at this time, the Japanese began kamikaze activities. This was a new ball game that required a shift in tactics, as we needed to shoot down *100 percent* of these kamikazes. *Jeep carriers* came into existence, loaded with fighters only. The big carriers added more fighters to their complement. During our training period with VMF-461, we lost three pilots in operational accidents.

We had a delightful visitor assigned to our squadron for three

*A few weeks earlier, the Allies landed in Normandy on June 6. D-Day opened up a second front against Germany in the European theatre of war.

weeks, Colonel Charles A. Lindbergh, who represented Chance Vought Aircraft, the manufacturer of the F4U-1D Corsair. He was a civilian pilot assigned to train us in the art of extending our flight range using the same amount of fuel. The key to preserve fuel on long flights is simply one of following the procedures set down by the colonel. When cruising altitude is attained, the pilot must lean back the gas mixture, a normal procedure already known and practiced, then pull the propeller pitch lever back from 2,750 RPMs to 1,750 RPMs and adjust the increased manifold pressure to about 38 inches of mercury. This would put you in a cruising speed of about 180 knots and give you maximum range with the fuel you carried. During flight training, we had been told that once airborne, we should throttle back from the 45 inches of mercury manifold pressure we pulled for take-off, and do it quickly before we blew the pistons. We realized that this high manifold pressure and high RPM (2,800) would do damage to the engine in prolonged periods of flight. But we did not know that a lower RPM would save fuel. During our long flights in the Corsair in days to come, we were to use this method taught us by Colonel Lindbergh.

Many men gave a lukewarm reception to this great pilot and hero of the first Atlantic solo crossing in 1927. Before the U.S. entry into the war, Charles Lindbergh's episode with the German Luftwaffe Command, in terms of the merits of the Me-109 in comparison with our own planes, was seen as pro-Nazi and as damaging to the industrial might of American industry.*

---

*After the U.S. entered the war, Lindbergh was eager to serve the Allied war effort. But an unforgiving President Roosevelt, who had reportedly vowed, "I'll clip that young man's wings," did not permit him to serve in the Army Air Corps. Nonetheless, Lindbergh eventually got to the South Pacific. As a technical adviser, he actually flew fifty combat missions, downing at least one Japanese fighter in a hair-raising dogfight.

But all along he was warning America of the advances Germany had made in fighter aircraft proven in combat over the skies of Spain. Feelings toward the Axis powers were strained during the thirties and Hitler's rise to power wasn't readily taken as menacing by many of our allies. Regardless, Colonel Lindbergh rendered a great service to the Marines stationed in El Centre.

One evening as I was returning from the Officers' Club, I saw Colonel Lindbergh walking back to his quarters, so I stopped to offer him a ride. He gladly hopped into my convertible and I was honored to drive him anywhere he wanted. He was very polite and thanked me for the ride as we made small talk. I asked why he wasn't assigned a special vehicle. He said he preferred it this way—a low profile. I regret to this day that I did not ask him to autograph my log book, which rested there on the dashboard. (This was my brand-new log book now that I had reached 1,000 hours of flight time.) But that's the way things go. After the war, I also had the opportunity to meet and "break bread" with Captain Eddie Rickenbacker. These two men, now deceased, were my heroes.

In November 1944, all squadron personnel were given leave in preparation for overseas assignment. I returned home and Louise and I became engaged. She accepted my ring and we made plans to be married as soon as I returned from this next combat tour. It was a date to which I looked forward. I was becoming anxious for this war to end. Louise would help me make the adjustment to civilian life.

Chapter 23

Second Overseas Tour

Upon my return to El Centre, we were informed that our group would not yet be assigned to carrier duties but would be sent to the Central Pacific to aid in neutralizing some of the islands that our forces had bypassed.* For the top echelon, this went over like a lead balloon. It would demoralize the members of our squadron. But we went to San Francisco and boarded another transport. The Golden Gate drifted past as we entered the Pacific. Seven days later, we anchored off the Diamond Head volcano in Hawaii. Although we were not allowed ashore, a few of us did manage to sneak off and visit Trader Vic's place. Returning aboard, we smuggled bottles of "fringe benefits" into our quarters. The rest of the voyage was more enjoyable.

At Eniwetok Atoll, we were told that our assignment would be the island of Engebi. We were on a small atoll with just enough place for a runway and living quarters. We were now in VMF-422. This squadron had a bad start in the war zone. It was detached from Midway on December 15, 1943, and went aboard the escort carrier *Kalinin Bay* with twenty-four new Corsairs on January 17, 1944. They were catapulted and landed

---

*General Douglas MacArthur's *withering vine* strategy. Our forces would bypass the strong points, cut off enemy supply lines, and let them "wither."

at Hawkins Field, Tarawa. On January 21,* they were ordered to fly the 700 miles to Funafuti Island with a stopover at Nanomea, 463 miles away. The C.O. did not request an escort plane. By January 25, twenty-three pilots of VMF-422 took off for Nanomea, following the Gilbert Islands as checkpoints. They ran into bad weather. Only one plane made it to Funafuti. This cost VMF-422 six pilots and twenty-two planes. This was the reason why we as a squadron were sidetracked to fill the vacancies. As this squadron had been assigned to the Marshall Islands, specifically Engebi, we arrived to finish their tour. We would proceed later to Okinawa.

The islands comprising the Eniwetok Atoll appeared on the rim of an elliptically shaped volcanic lip protruding a few feet above the Pacific Ocean. The center of the lagoon was very deep, with a harbor entrance found only at Eniwetok. Engebi proved to be a "vacation" for us old pilots. Every week we would make a flying strike with 2,000-pound bombs on the Japanese-held island of Ponape. We would fly the 367 miles to Ponape, using Ujelang Atoll as a checkpoint. Ponape was close to Truk, the "Japanese Pearl Harbor." Twenty-four of our planes would make a dive-bombing run of the enemy airfield. We would lower the wheels of our Corsairs for stability and push down from 12,000 feet, retracting the wheels as we pulled out of our dive. Sometimes we would dive clean, but this would only generate more speed and less accuracy. Jug Herlihy usually led the bombing run, followed by my division. We would blow holes in the runways, but the Japanese would cover them up again. This was repeated on a weekly basis over and over again. I have never seen a more beautiful island in the Pacific than Ponape.

*On December 16 of the previous month, the Germans made a desperate last-ditch attempt at victory, the Battle of the Bulge.

One could see sunken "cities" among the coral reefs. Intelligence had it that a German officer lived on the island before the war and had a huge refrigeration ice plant functioning there. We searched for it solely to bomb it out of existence. On one corner of the island was a large lighthouse, the target of many of our pull-out runs.

It was during this tour that my earlier training in photo school was put to use. Strike Command wanted damage assessment after each strike. A Corsair was rigged with a floor camera. Because my record reflected an MOS in photo, I was stuck with the job. I would separate from the rest of the fighters for the photo run, which required me to maintain an altitude of 3,000 feet while taking a heading that would bring me directly over the bombed runways. I would throw a switch that opened a trapdoor, exposing the lens. When the nose of my fighter crossed the runway below, I would throw another switch that put in motion the camera's film. From then on, I would be a sitting duck for the AA gunners, so I would call on eight fighters to make strafing passes, keeping the enemy's gunners busy while I did my thing. Needless to say, I cursed the day I put my name in the ring for photo school. *Never again.* I never received any arrows, but these flights felt like an eternity. Many a flight to home base was made with my camera grinding away, camera doors inadvertently left open. I would use more fuel with this extra flight drag, but the Corsair had a good reserve.

When we were not flying missions, this time period became unexciting and wearying for us. We always looked forward to U.S. holidays, even Halloween! As I mentioned before, the best foods were on Navy ships, so we'd supplement our supply by scrounging. We'd sometimes receive packages and special foods, such as turkey for Thanksgiving and fruitcake for

Christmas. Our imaginations made the celebrations more festive, with special clothing, props, and food.

During this "vacation," we pilots had lots of time to mix with the command personnel of our squadron. Captain William Fontaine Alexander, an insurance magnate from Dallas who was our intelligence officer, provided us with current data. We shared the same tent quarters. Quite often I would return from a flight to see a blue envelope on my cot, a letter from Louise, which he had picked up for me from the mail room. Another close friend was Captain John Reynolds, our engineering officer. Captain Reynolds was highly respected by the pilots of VMF-422. We always had confidence in our engines, which he supervised, when we made the runs to Ponape. Both men contributed much to the success of our combat action at this time and in the Okinawa campaign. Regrettably, Fontaine was killed many years after the war in an airline crash between Houston and Dallas. John Reynolds, who passed away a few years ago, was an attorney in Alabama.

We encountered no fighter action, but soon the war was becoming more aggressive. The MacArthur, King, and Roosevelt meeting at Pearl Harbor was, of course, unknown to us. Although General MacArthur got his wish for a return to the Philippines, Admiral King got us into the Iwo Jima-Okinawa area, a move that shortened the war. We only knew the little picture.

We had so much time on our hands that Lieutenant Kopas, who was an artist, suggested pictures for our planes. He had the "Thundering Hog" painted on the cowling of a squadron plane. There was painted on another plane a Frenchman crying out "Touché" as he severed with his sword the head of a Japanese. I had not requested this, but someone remembered my speaking about Alcibiades' Gettysburg campaign. Of course, women were a popular theme in fuselage art.

We often flew to other islands in our utility SNJ or SBD two-passenger aircraft. One morning, one of our pilots was elected to trade movies with another island. We threw a bucket of cold water on him to get him out of the sack as we had had a later party the previous night. It was his turn to fly this "mission." He struggled out of bed, put on his helmet and goggles, grabbed the canisters of film, and proceeded to the flight line. He noticed a passenger in the rear seat, a young private. This was customary, as many troops wanted a hop to kill the island doldrums. The pilot signed the yellow acceptance sheet, started the engine, and taxied out. He swung the aircraft into the wind, revved up the engine, checked the magnetos, throttled back, and leaned over the side as he upchucked the contents of his stomach. The man in the rear seat was gone by the time he poured the coal to the engine. He completed the flight with no problems. I think that the young private in the rear seat missed a good flight.

Chapter 24

Okinawa

VMF-422 headed for the forward war zone on May 16, 1945.* The first leg would be a thousand-mile flight over water to Tinian Island in the Caroline chain. With three external tanks, two internal ones, and the main tank, the trip would be well within the range of the Corsair, using the procedures Lindbergh taught us. The only hitch would be the eight and one-half hours in a cramped cockpit, flying wing on an escort DC-3. We landed in Tinian late on the afternoon of the 16th. May 17 would be a day of rest.

I had received a letter from home telling me that my first cousin, Sergeant Robert Judice, was on Guam with a B-29 outfit. On May 17, I hopped a ride to Guam in a worn-out DC-3.** We barely made it off the airfield, which was littered with the debris of wrecked Japanese planes. I vowed never again to take such foolish chances. Nonetheless, I got to see Robert. We

*By this time, the war in Europe was over, marked by V-E Day, May 8, 1945! The Russian army had entered Berlin, trapping Adolf Hitler in his bunker. Hitler committed suicide on April 30, 1945. Germany surrendered unconditionally to the Allies on May 7 at Reims, France. In that momentous spring, President Franklin Roosevelt had died of natural causes on April 12. Vice-President Harry S. Truman became the nation's thirty-third president.

**Over fifty years later (1997), after the island of Guam was decimated by Supertyphoon Paka, my son Richard would fly there to lend a helping hand. Richard was born, by the way, on Pearl Harbor Day (December 7), 1953.

spent a few hours visiting and exchanging news about the folks back home. At about 1500 hours (3:00 PM), I returned to Tinian for a good night's rest.

The flight to Iwo Jima, our second leg, took only about five hours, but it was in bad weather. We stayed the night on Iwo and witnessed a strategically senseless night-fighter action, which resulted in the downing of two Japanese Betty bombers (Iwo had fallen into American hands on March 17, 1945). One made a crash landing close to our fighters, which were neatly lined on the runway. The next morning we saw firsthand and examined the remains of the Japanese crew in the wreckage. It's amazing how human beings can function in the midst of man's inhumanity to man. Witnessing such carnage did not affect our appetites!

After a quick breakfast, we manned our planes for the last leg into Okinawa. We were airborne for over nine hours, flying on instruments for four hours. I thought we were over the China coast by this time, but we weren't. We temporarily lost two of our boys in the soupy weather, but they managed to preserve the correct heading and picked up our formation as we broke out for a few minutes into clear weather. We were back on the gauges and our escort DC-3 was guiding our descent through the overcast. We broke out of the overcast at about 300 feet right over Naha, the capital of Okinawa and the center of fighting. My fighter was the only one to pick up arrows from the fighting. What a welcome for me! We broke off from our escort and I was the first to land on the island of Ie Shima, where the celebrated journalist and war correspondent Ernie Pyle had been killed a few weeks before.

Orientation flights were a thing of the past. Our squadron flew with the usual maps strapped onto our right knee pad for orientation. The situation here reminded me of the Solomon Islands. We would be flying in a hostile area surrounded by Japanese airfields, occupied China to the west, and the vast Pacific Ocean to the east. The weather here was as bad as in the Solomons, and the winds were of greater velocity.

Ie Shima was an ideal "carrier type" island, elevated out of the South China Sea with a mesa rising 450 feet above sea level. The rise resembled a carrier launch platform. We would have to keep this in mind during instrument conditions. Major Tex Dew selected as our living area the ridge overlooking the northern part of the island. Tents, with foxholes dug inside, were set up on the skyline of the ridge. Although we had many air raids, I never used the foxhole. I guess my brain was programmed from Guadalcanal days to use foxholes only during shellings. I had developed a false sense of security about what was or wasn't danger.

This was not a six-week fighting tour but a period of steady alert. We were on the offensive. The workload was distributed among many fighter squadrons. Tactics had changed to meet the new kamikaze threat. For two hours at a time, we simply flew a four-plane CAP patrol (Combat Air Patrol) at 10,000 feet to protect potential American targets from the Japanese. It was very monotonous. To put spice into the routine, we would radio the destroyer personnel below, often communicating with them in code, "Red Dog One to Fleet Two," for instance.

I decided to drop down one day to check the deck of a certain destroyer over which we were flying cover. I checked with Okinawa control for any possible radar blips on the 175-mile scan and received a negative. I radioed the other three fighters in my division to remain on station, as I peeled off in a screaming dive for the surface. I radioed the destroyer about my actions and approached with caution. The gunners were trigger-happy and nervous. I flew about ten feet above the water, on the same course as the "can." To my surprise, I saw a large sign on the directrix panel that read, "This way to the carriers." It was meant for the kamikaze pilots, not for me. I waggled my wings and started climbing back on station to lead my flight. I no longer flew wing but was a division leader and soon would lead forty-five fighters into action.

This dive to the surface would be remembered forty-three years later when I was a guest of a destroyer crew in a September 1988 reunion in Baton Rouge, Louisiana. I went aboard the U.S.S. *Brush* that may have been in the area, and my name was entered on the record of the ship's complement.

As already mentioned, our Fighter Command used four fighters in two-hour shifts to fly CAP patrol over destroyers. These destroyers, placed as the numbers on a clock, formed a ring around Okinawa. Looking north from Okinawa was the twelve o'clock position, from which the other positions followed in a clockwise fashion. Marine fighter squadrons would be assigned to fly over each destroyer in the picket patrol. The Army Air Corps (as it was known at that time) would send P-51 fighters to escort B-29 strikes against the Japanese mainland.

At about 1400 hours (2:00 PM) on May 28, two divisions of planes were flying patrol over Amami-O-Shima. One was led by Major Chris Lee and the other by me. We spotted a dozen or so kamikaze planes flying at about 4,000 feet below us. It looked to me like a trap, as I had flashbacks to the old days. I sent Lieutenant Allison and Lieutenant Snapper down to engage them with their respective wingmen, while we kept the high altitude for any surprises. I scanned the skies for enemy fighters but saw none. By this time, our fighters had made contact and were shooting down enemy planes like flies. I dropped down to get into the action. Both Lieutenant Snapper and Lieutenant Barnes had burned three each, and Barnes said that he drove another into the water. In the old days we didn't get credit for this type of action, but maybe they did on this front. I do not know. Regardless, by the time my division reached the action, three of us managed to get one each. The one I fired on was so close that I overshot and quickly skidded away as we glanced at each other in passing. The Japanese pilot was wearing a black ceremonial outfit complete with goggles. I was now in front of his guns! (But kamikaze pilots were not a threat as their planes carried huge bombs which prevented their dogfighting. They were sitting ducks in combat. Their only purpose was to crash dive on our ships to a certain death.) I swiftly pulled away at high speed and winged over for a head-on shot. He crashed into the China Sea. We formed up and went back to Angels 10 (10,000 feet) for routine orbits. After we landed, attention was drawn to Lieutenant Snapper's plane. He had fired at such a close range that he flew through flames that badly seared his right wing, drawing many favorable comments from the line crew. Such a daring pilot!

Kamikaze pilots were not the only strategy. In desperation, the Japanese sent a convoy of ships, led by the colossal battleship *Yamato,* toward Okinawa. The *Yamato* surpassed even the German battleship *Bismarck!* The ships had only enough fuel for a one-way trip. Even this fuel was of poor quality. Toward the end of the war, Japan was reduced to refueling with unrefined petroleum, which produced volatile, explosive vapors.

The convoy was to run aground on Okinawa's beaches, becoming giant pillboxes. The crew would then rush to the aid of their entrenched comrades. But the convoy was intercepted far out at sea by our carrier planes. Most of the ships, including the *Yamato,* were sunk. This foolish effort by the once-proud Imperial Navy cost the lives of over thirty-six hundred Japanese.

The month of June was uneventful for us. Alternately, our ground forces launched the final assault on the Japanese defense line in the south. Surmounting stiff enemy resistance, Okinawa was finally declared secured on June 22. Sadly, General Simon Buckner, U.S. Tenth Army Commander, did not live to see the victory. He was killed on June 18 by artillery fire while in a forward position with the assault infantry. We flew on strike missions and on picket patrol over destroyers from dawn until dusk. Finally, we were ordered off Ie Shima island to Okinawa, first to Kadena Airfield then to Chimu. We remained here until the war ended. We dropped napalm bombs on Japanese lines and fired many rockets at smoke-marked positions.

Of course there were parties. We had a regular flight connection with Pearl Harbor. There were no shortages of food and other party items. I wanted a pair of Japanese binoculars, and one day an enterprising private from the front lines made the rounds of our flight quarters for trading purposes. I gave him two fifths of Old Taylor in exchange for a beautiful pair of field lenses. He traded with many of the other pilots, but unknown to us, his pal would rob our quarters when we were on flights. So although I hid my treasure, the "spy" found them and made off with the items from another "sucker pilot." *C'est la vie!* That's life!

During lulls in the fighting, we occasionally had time to spare. Fighter squadrons were widespread and missions were on a time-allotted basis. We were situated near an old sugar beet plantation on Okinawa, but the machinery had been bombed out long ago. I checked out in a torpedo bomber for extra flight time and also to have a spare craft to fly around visiting friends.

Among my visitors was Octave Gutekunst, my first cousin, whom I had not seen since college days. He dropped in one day clear out of nowhere. He was a corporal in Army intelligence (tested with a high I.Q.) and had just arrived on Okinawa. Through our local town newspaper and letters from home, he obtained my whereabouts. We had a nice chat and he stayed over for a day. Since he had to report back the next day to the vicinity of Naha, he asked if I could get a jeep and drive him back to his company. I quickly informed Octave that even though Okinawa was in American hands, there were many concealed resistance groups. I further pointed out that it was over twenty miles to Naha, over a route where three of our Marines had been bushwhacked. I wasn't about ready to be picked off this late in the war by a Japanese guerilla sniper. After mentioning how dangerous it was to be a foot soldier, I told him that I would fly him over to Naha after giving him a tour of the islands where we fought. He was game and I put him in the ball turret of the torpedo bomber and off we went. My log book records the date as July 29, 1945, with total flight time of 2.5 hours. We landed at Naha and parted company. Later, on September 24, I was visited by Sergeant R. L. Thomas and his friend E. L. Jasper. Since R. L. was from the old hometown, I took both him and his friend up in the torpedo bomber, the TBM-3,* placing R. L. in the ball turret and his friend in the tail stinger gunner's position for a "tour" of the war zone.

One of the operations officers, who had flight time only in utility aircraft, decided that he wanted to check out in the Corsair. In peacetime, he could not have done this without the usual precautions. Although the fighter is rather easy to fly, one

*The TBM-3 was the type of aircraft flown in World War II by George H. W. Bush, who became our nation's forty-first president. I would later meet him.

must allow for proper flight time and experience. Well, this officer got in and started to taxi. After the tail of the aircraft lifted off, he panicked and hit the brakes. Perhaps he was not properly squared away with the runway or maybe the tail didn't lift fast enough for him to orient the roll-out run. Regardless, the act of stomping on the brakes caused the craft to nose up and flip over on its back, rupturing the 100-octane gas tank and spilling raw gasoline over the runway. He was strapped in his seat with a closed canopy overhead. In this inverted position, he didn't stand a chance if the fumes were to ignite. Lucky for him, we reached the scene and quickly formed a ring around the plane to prevent onlookers from entering the area with lighted cigarettes. We held our breath as a crane lifted the aircraft which was still inverted, while we slid the canopy back and unbuckled the pilot who fell out head first. He was fortunate.

Chapter 25

A Jinx from the Past

The twenty-ninth of June proved to be a bad day for pilots of VMF-422, a jinx still hanging on from the past. I had no way of knowing that this day would be one of my last close encounters with death. We were briefed the evening before about a new type of bomb fuse known as the VT fuse. Since kamikaze action had all but ceased in our area, our squadron had been engaged, before June 21, in close air support of our ground troops on Okinawa. We would strap onto our aircraft napalm (fire bombs) and eight five-inch rockets. One of our aviators would be sent to the front lines where he established radio communications with our flight leader. Once the target had been selected and identified with the proper color of smoke for that day, we would drop out of the sky from orbiting positions and smoke up the area. It was a foolproof method. We were thoroughly trained in this capacity because close air support is one of the main functions of Marine aviation.

Getting back to my briefing about the VT fuse bomb, we were told that under no circumstances were we to drop this ordnance over land until we were on target. This highly secret fuse was top level security and must not fall into Japanese hands. After its release from the aircraft, the fuse armed the bomb when its nose propeller turned 300 revolutions. A signal would be emitted forward, striking the ground and reflecting back to the bomb causing it to explode above ground in a downward and sideward burst of shrapnel, destroying planes and personnel in foxholes. In other words, it was a proximity fuse.

There is a parallel between the coming mission and that of Project *Aphrodite* in Europe which resulted in the death of Lieutenant Joseph Kennedy. Kennedy was a Navy pilot stationed in England, flying the PB4Y-1, a Navy version of the B-24. The project was in the experimental stages. Networks of electronic switches were used to control drones (pilotless planes) loaded with high explosive bombs. These drones, guided electronically by a mother aircraft, would then be flown "kamikaze fashion" into the German submarine pens off the coast of France. The only hitch in the plan was the take-off stage, wheels retraction, and flying the plane to an altitude where the mother ship could take over the controls and guide the drone into the target. A pilot and a radio electronics expert were needed for these functions. When the proper altitude was reached, both the pilot and the radio electronics expert would parachute out of the craft and the mother ship would take control of the drone. Lieutenant Joe Kennedy and Bud Willy flew on the first such mission. Before they bailed out, a final switch arming the bombs would have to be thrown. An electronic defect in this switch accidentally triggered the explosion which tragically killed both Kennedy and Willy.* The pilots of VMF-422 were to experience a similar series of incidences. This is the price a nation pays for rapidly changing combat situations. Safety comes last! The use of the VT fuse reflects an all-out effort against a ruthless, fanatical enemy.

To better understand this behavior, it should be noted that

*Lieutenant Joseph Kennedy was being groomed to run for President of the United States.

many of the Japanese soldiers seemed to be tough and fatalistic. Their training taught them that they were invincible. Yet in reality, these same troops lacked individual initiative and, although tenacious in defense, had a tendency to unnecessarily choose death rather than retreat or surrender. Emphasis was given to the idea that the soldier's life belonged to the emperor and thus it was deemed a great honor to die for him and a greater shame to surrender no matter what the odds.

I led forty-five fighters and Major Chris Lee another group of forty-five. But on this mission only VMF-422 pilots had rockets and VT fuse bombs. All other fighters carried standard bombs and napalm. In keeping with the jinx, the weather was not too favorable and our rendezvous point, twenty miles away at 10,000 feet, might also be in inclement weather. Since most of the ninety fighters were from different fields and carriers, we had to make this a well-coordinated effort. I was assigned my old aircraft, the Frenchman crying out "Touché" on the cowling. I checked out the aircraft visually, a standard procedure, and started to strap in the cockpit when I noticed a jeep being driven in my direction. An officer jumped on my wing and informed me that as leader of the first forty-five aircraft, I had to take plane number 44. I was short-tempered in my reply, stating that we had radio contact and, anyhow, how could they read numbers in flight? He was insistent, so I unstrapped and, with my parachute still on, climbed into the jeep. I was driven to another fighter, and started the engine after signing the yellow sheet of acceptance. I didn't bother to visibly check this plane. We were late in getting away from the flight line.

I finally got behind one Army P-47 and would be next for takeoff. The P-47 was shaped like a jug and looked like a bumble bee. I wondered how such a craft could fly. It was a plane well suited for combat in Europe and in the Pacific. I noticed that the pilot didn't clear his engine, but simply lined up with the runway and started to roll. An engine will load up and lose power on take-off if the carbon isn't burnt off by clearing the engine with high RPM and high manifold pressure, then quickly changing the propeller to fine pitch, which burns off the impurities collected during taxiing. Well, the P-47 didn't get airborne and crashed at the end of the runway where it caught fire. We had to drop 15 degrees of flaps in order to clear the wreck and fire-fighting equipment. I had a feeling of doom I could not shake as I set the course for my rendezvous with the others. As we came on station for the join-up, the sun broke out of the clouds and I began to feel better about the whole flight objective.

I contacted Chris Lee on the proper channel and we joined forces for the trip to Ishigaki Island in the southern chain of the Ryukyus. Our objective was to neutralize an airfield where the Japanese were sending planes from China to hit our rear. With this strike force, we would probably sink the island. Twenty minutes from our objective, all hell broke loose. I thought we had been hit by Japanese fighters. Two of our planes blew up in midair. I found out later that the first plane to burst was the one I had just vacated when told to change. Lieutenant Greene (for reasons of my own I will not give his real name) was flying this plane with Lieutenant Hale on his wing. Both men perished. Immediately, the radio silence usually kept on all missions was violated with oaths about those bombs we were carrying. We were over water and I immediately ordered all fighters to jettison "Big Sting," the code name for the VT fuse weapon. As I repeated the order over the radio, I dropped mine along with my extra fuel tanks in the excitement. Although I had dropped my extra gas tanks, I knew I could complete the mission with the fuel I had left.

I began to appreciate my quick decision and reaction time, when I noticed with horror that my second section didn't drop as ordered. I quickly informed them to drop the bombs. We would go in with our rockets. We were still over water, approaching our island objective, but both Lieutenant Landsberg and Lieutenant Stevenson unaccountably didn't acknowledge my command. Both simply grinned at me. I knew they witnessed our drops because they were in my flight of four planes, below my flight path, and had to be looking my way since we were flying close formation. I radioed the other flight leader that two of my men had not succeeded in dropping the VT fuse bombs and that I would investigate. Lieutenant Beha from Watertown, New York, was flying my wing and remained on course as I dropped below and flew under Lieutenant Landsberg's fighter and looked at the VT fuse linkage. All seemed okay. I flew under Lieutenant Stevenson's plane and again all seemed in order. I slid back in position and told them to remain aloft and not, repeat, not follow us down but release their bombs immediately. By this time, the rest of the planes were in position and were calling for completion of the mission, as some of the planes were not Corsairs and didn't have the range we had.

I repeated my orders to Lieutenant Landsberg and Lieutenant Stevenson and received "rogers" from both. As flight leader, I was the first to dive. This was to be a double dive, the bombs on the first pass and the rockets on the second. I completed a dummy first run, and watched as all the others went through the first run. I had climbed up for the second pass and got into position when I heard someone yell over the radio that antiaircraft fire had struck two of our fighters. I looked around and saw far below two fading puffs of dense smoke. As I started my rocket run, I didn't notice any heavy AA fire and pulled out with the intention of setting the stage for the rendezvous to head home. I failed to see my second section during the rendezvous. Lieutenant Beha was already locked in on my wing, but Lieutenant Landsberg and Lieutenant Stevenson were absent from the second section slot. I called for them during the join up period, but failed to get an answer. I realized what might have happened. But how could this have been possible? I was in radio contact with them. They knew what was going on. Yet, they were gone. What happened?

Upon our return and debriefing, we got some inkling into the series of errors causing this wartime accident.* One of the factors had to do with the wiring of the safety fuse linkage. Instead of the safety fuse wiring being in line with the flight path of the plane, it was anchored to a pylon a few degrees off the flight path. This could have caused the safety wire to work loose in the slipstream, which would have pulled the wire out of the linkage holder, freeing the bomb's propeller to turn in the wind. After 300 revolutions, the impulse would have been emitted, striking the Corsair's propeller, reflecting back to the bomb, and triggering it. This was a possibility. One of our fighters, which was loaded with the VT fuse bomb, failed to get off

*Samuel Hynes, in his book *Flights of Passage,* mentions this flight to Ishigaki, but although he was on the flight I was leading, he didn't receive all the information. Only four fighters were destroyed. Three of the arming wires had worked loose in flight, causing the bombs' propellers to rotate freely in the wind. After 300 revolutions, the bomb was armed and sent an impulse m line with the bomb's flight path. But the Corsair's *propeller* reflected the impulse back to the bomb, causing the proximity bomb to explode. This happened in three planes, while the fourth blew up because he was flying close wing on the first plane to explode. The Corsair's propeller is thirteen feet, four and one quarter inches in diameter and was directly in the flight path of the bombs, forming a reflective surface for the emitted impulse. In his book, Hynes wrote that the impulse was reflected from other aircraft.

and was still in the revetment when we returned. This gave us information that helped us determine the probable cause.

I spent the next few days testing, in dives of 300 knots, dummy bombs with different fuse linkage wiring positions to see if the linkage would work loose. The only one which did not work loose was the one wired in line with the flight path of the aircraft. Nevertheless, during subsequent strike missions, many of the line personnel would shy away from the taxi strip whenever we would pass by with the VT fuse bombs, especially when we carried napalm. The loss of these two fine fighter pilots in my division affected me. Although I have built a barrier around my associations with fellow pilots (we all do), that day has haunted me and will continue to do so for the rest of my life.

Chapter 26

The Atomic Bomb

During the first sixteen days of August, there was a nightmare of vectors to "blips" on the radar screen which didn't make sense in 1945. I was on a morning flight with my division and was to report as usual on station for the two-hour picket patrol over a destroyer at the seven o'clock location. I suddenly received a frantic call from Control to buster (aviation terminology for "full speed") to a target at 25,000 feet. We were just climbing through 5,000 feet and I had to drop the full belly tank* in order to climb rapidly to intercept this enemy. The vector was perfect and I arrived at 25,000 feet in seconds, but there was no enemy. The radar operators said my target was just about a mile ahead. I charged the guns and rockets, looked ahead, but saw nothing. Just then the radar operators said the target was pulling away at high speed and asked me to advance speed to intercept. The blip was off the radar screen in seconds. Nothing we had in those days could travel the full length of a radar screen at that velocity. I laughed and told the operator to stop watching flies on his screen. I even suggested that he check for a leaky capacitor in the horizontal circuit of his scope. This was my first and last encounter with UFOs. After August 16, we were not plagued with anymore sightings of this

*Corsairs had belly tanks at this time.

nature. All vectors were normal and within the range and velocity of World War II aircraft.

For almost twenty days, our squadron was involved in attacks on Japan itself. We had specific targets to strafe on Kyushu, one of the islands of the Japanese mainland. On August 5, 1945, we were suddenly and unexpectedly ordered to stop striking Kyushu. We could not understand the logic of Fighter Command. After all, we had successfully blasted the numerous airfields there for many days. Surely it would be unwise not to continue since we had succeeded in neutralizing enemy air power over this southernmost island of Japan's mainland. Also, we knew that we could soften the beachheads for the future invasion of Japan. The following day, August 6, answered all our questions and gripes. A new type of bomb was dropped on Hiroshima and another on Nagasaki on August 9,* introducing a new method of warfare, the "atomic era," which ushered in the Cold War!

It was difficult for us to believe that such a weapon existed and we had to verify it for ourselves. Many of us wanted to fly over the bombed-out cities, but were denied permission. The clouds of debris remained suspended in the air for a while after the blast. Needless to say, this brought the Japanese to the bargaining table and the subsequent ending of World War II. It also brought back memories of my college physics classes. Professor Lawrence of Cal. Tech. had said that whoever splits the atom will control the world in the palm of his hand.

It is well to note that the Japanese were in bad shape before this bomb was dropped. Our submarines had cut off all shipping to Japan. The B-29s were systematically pulverizing city after city on the mainland. We had air superiority. It was just a

---

*In the construction of an atomic weapon, two must be made by the very nature of the atomic table.

matter of time before we invaded. It would have been bloody, for the Japanese were arming all sorts of kamikazes to be used against our invasion forces. Surely the decision to drop the atomic bomb saved many American lives.*

---

*When President Harry S. Truman gave the order to the Joint Chiefs of Staff to go ahead with this action, all branches of the Armed forces were involved. The Army Air Corps made the drop from a B-29, the *Enola Gay*.

Chapter 27

The Good Old U.S.A.

One could sense the winding down of the war. On September 1, we received new Corsairs, F4U-4s, which were an improvement over the F4U-lDs. They had a better cockpit seating arrangement with a floorboard, added horsepower, and fuel switches that enabled us to siphon fuel from external sources and internal wing tanks to our main tank. It also had a four-bladed propeller. Gone was the chasm staring one in the face as one looked down the "well" of the Corsair. The floor panel gave one a sense of space flight, with the console of gasoline transfer switches at the pilot's fingertips. Two 20mm cannon were added to the firepower of this Corsair.

Unbeknownst to us, the new Corsairs were already obsolete, despite their great advancement. They could be described as another so-called "technological dead end"! A great technological leap would supplant this new, improved aircraft. *Jet propulsion,* the rearward discharge of hot, compressed air and exhaust gases to produce forward propulsion, would make the propeller "prop" plane antiquated and destined for the scrapheap, museums, or air shows.*

On September 2, 1945, Japan formally surrendered aboard

*Resourcefully, propellers would make a limited comeback in the form of turboprop planes. These planes are pulled swiftly through the air by propellers, the propellers themselves being driven by a smooth-turning jet turbine.

the battleship *Missouri* anchored in Tokyo Bay. The war had finally ended and we were placed on surveillance flights. The war might be over, but we still faced in the area a fanatical enemy with kamikaze abilities.

During this interim, our C.O., Major Tex Dew, informed us that reserve officers would not receive flight pay anymore, since flight duty would be taken over by regular Marine officers. Like the previous injustices, this one also went over like a lead balloon. All reserve pilots simply refused to fly. Hanging up helmets and goggles was the order of the day. At the same time, a drive was made to bring as many reserve pilots as possible into the regular Marine Corps. This was a feeble, poorly planned attempt by a group of officers. They called all reserve pilots to headquarters and lectured us on World War I statistics, that is, how returning veterans had been selling pencils on street corners after the war. This negative approach only succeeded in alienating the reserve pilots from the regular ones. Anyhow, the regular Marines were definitely in the minority. I again recalled Rudyard Kipling's *Tommy*. What a brilliant man Kipling was! Many of his writings were still applicable to the situations of World War II, especially *Gunga Din* and *Mandalay*.

Enough is enough! A few of us spoke to the group, stating that all pilots who signed up before December 7, 1941, were entitled to a mustering out bonus of $500 a year for every year served, up to four years. If they were now to transfer to the regular Marine Corps, they would forfeit this bonus. This had been a package deal in the Aviation Cadet V-5 program ("Clause J") in order to recruit pilots so desperately needed during the dark days of 1941.

They are ideal for serving routes of less than 500 miles, as the short distance and flight time makes it impractical to climb to high altitudes where the standard jet engine is most efficient.

The next day we were informed that flight pay had been restored to reserve pilots, and we were back on patrol. I'm sure some officer's rank remained the same or was lowered because of this. It is axiomatic that wars are made up of troops from civilian life as well as reserves, with career personnel who have the savvy to mold everyone into a fighting force. I wanted to remain a part of this force on a reserve basis, since the Marine Corps had been good to me over the years.

It was exciting to fly at low altitudes over Japan and look over the targets at which I had shot in high-speed dives and evasive tactics. Now with the advent of peace, a complacent attitude prevailed. I even touched my wheels on an airfield in Japan and bounced back into the air without landing as a gesture of defiance. Although I would not be in the occupation forces moving in, I could not see fighting the Japanese for four years and not "landing" on their soil. It was a weird feeling, especially as this was one of the very airfields I had strafed only days before. Maybe this was pushing my luck, but at twenty-four years of age, I still had a little daring left.

The day arrived. Our nation would start to demobilize. A point system, for return to the States and mustering out of military personnel, was set up. Points were given for years and days in the service, medals earned while in action, and other items that I cannot recall at this time. But the ringer was *age*. All men thirty-five years and older were given the green light for immediate return with high priority. At twenty-four years of age, I could not see the wisdom of this. I wanted to return and get married to Louise, so I began to look for loopholes in the system. It didn't take long to find them. Who could keep track of this movement? *Nobody*. We did not have computers in those days. It was always a question of typed orders and "ten" copies for distribution.

As soon as we became detached from flying duties with VMF-422, many of us began to look for space available on flights to Pearl Harbor. A few of us beat, by days, typhoon weather in Okinawa. I got a flight via Guam on the old workhorse DC-3 to Hawaii. Upon arrival, we were informed that our stay in Pearl Harbor would be over a month, before we could even be considered for passage to the mainland. This was the Pacific bottleneck, the converging station for all points west and east. After two days around the swimming pool and beaches of Hawaii, I had enough. It was then that we received word that the Third Fleet would be entering Pearl Harbor, in preparation for its victorious run to the continental United States. This was it! My outlet to the good old United States. Hadn't we flown picket patrol over the destroyers stationed around Okinawa?

I waited until the fleet officers were on shore and that evening I struck out for the Naval Officers' Club in the docking area. As we all know, officers in the Navy as well as in other branches polarize at the bar. Pilots stick together, destroyer officers stick together, and so on. I waited until the party was in full swing before I jumped on a table and said, "Red Dog One, this is Eagle One; we are on station with four chicks and holding at Angels 10." I was going through the radio procedure of coming on picket patrol over the destroyers at 10,000 feet with a flight of four Corsairs. My Louisiana accent was recognized almost immediately by someone over in a wing of the club. These Navy guys certainly knew how to throw a party. I couldn't buy a round and the stories were flying fast and furious. They let me know that I was almost shot down the day I buzzed a destroyer near Okinawa. It was a great reunion. After a while, I spoke about "booking passage" with them as they were leaving in the morning. "Do you have orders?" one officer said. "No," I replied, "but show me a typewriter and I'll have some in twenty minutes." Then it dawned on me—why not? Who could possibly trace this in the mass of paperwork? By the time it could be verified, I would be home. I was ushered to a typewriter and started to type a most beautiful set of orders transferring me from the pool of waiting personnel in Hawaii to the Third Fleet and the destroyer U.S.S. *Brush* (DD-745) with quarters to be the hammock in the fighter director chart room. I didn't finish typing the orders. I chickened out. The officer in command was Commander John Victor Smith, U.S.N. He saw to it that my orders were issued. I was on my way. I returned to my quarters in Pearl to pick up my things, returned to the destroyer base, and got aboard ship that night.

We sailed the next day for Bremerton, Washington. The seven days back were relaxing and I managed to get a haircut and observe life aboard a destroyer. I didn't envy these men's position under war conditions, yet I could tell how dedicated they were to this type of duty. *Chaque à son goût.* To each his own. Little did I know that the orders I cut would catch up with me. In 1988, I received a letter inviting me to a reunion of all men who fought aboard the *DD-745*, as my name was found among the list of those aboard this destroyer during the 1945 era. I quickly replied that I was not a Navy man, but a Marine, and gave the details of my short Navy career on the *Brush*. Well, they made me an honorary sailor. Although I hadn't attended any reunion of this group before, I went in 1988 to their Fourth Annual Reunion in Baton Rouge, Louisiana. I guess everything in life done out of line will surface one day. It was refreshing to break bread with some of the plank officers and men I had been associated with forty-three years before.

I was at last separated in Bremerton and was on my way to

Louisiana. Louise and I were married on November 18, 1945, and today we enjoy remembering that era. We have five children (one daughter and four sons), seven grandchildren, and two great-grandchildren. Our daughter is Barbara DeBlanc Romero, an elementary-school teacher, married to Tommy Romero. Our oldest son, Jeff Jr., is a Roman Catholic priest who studied in Rome, Italy, before his ordination. We were fortunate to be with him in Europe during the period I taught in the DOD school systems there from 1974 to 1979. Our three other sons are Richard, a free agent, married to Irma Chavez (from Brownsville, Texas: full circle again to the Southwest); Frank, a civil engineer who married Margaret Guidry; and Michael, also a civil engineer who married Pamela Roy.

It was a bit difficult for me to adjust to civilian life again after my war experiences. At twenty-four years of age, I had had many responsible tasks as a captain in the Marines. Now I was merged with the general population. So, I returned to college, under the G.I. Bill of Rights program, and obtained a degree in science and mathematics from the College of Liberal Arts at S.L.I. I didn't adjust readily to one particular lifestyle. I thought of entering politics but quickly knew this was not my field. I finally entered the teaching profession, settled down, and enjoyed every minute of it. This was my purpose in life and although I had my ups and downs it was, for me, a good choice.

I had been awarded the Navy Cross for action in the Solomons, which I wore proudly from 1943 to 1945. But, on December 6, 1946, I was again ordered to active duty. The Navy Cross was revoked and President Harry S. Truman presented me the Medal of Honor, in a ceremony at the White House. It appears that I had been recommended for the Medal of Honor back in 1943, but after this action was endorsed by Admiral

Halsey, with Admiral King's approval, the process was put on hold until after the war. In the meantime, the Navy Cross was approved for the action of January 31, 1943.

I remained in the Marine Reserve program from 1946 to 1972. Although I did not complete thirty years, I did manage to get over twenty years of satisfactory service. I enjoyed every year with the Corps and retired as a colonel.

During the 1990s, I returned three times* to the Solomon Islands. These visits, including the ceremonies commemorating the fiftieth anniversary of the Battle of Guadalcanal, are covered in part 3 of this book. I also give an account of the genesis of the Battle of Guadalcanal and Solomon Islands Foundation, the brainchild of Major Bill Fisher, which endeavors to preserve Guadalcanal's battle sites for future generations. My son Richard's experiences in the Vietnam War are likewise noted. There is finally a description of the reunion of some old friends mentioned in this narrative.

As I conclude this part of my book, I want to say that the officers and men of VMF-112, the other Cactus Air Force squadrons, and VMF-422 were a good sampling of what America had to offer. When the chips were down, during the dark days of the war and in its final countdown days of the kamikaze, they gave their best for our country. I would like to say that the world will never again see the likes of these men. But I have faith in future generations of our fighters. Maybe the world will be "young" for them as it had been for us on Guadalcanal and Okinawa. The words of Captain Tex Jordan (the intelligence officer of VMF-113), "and we knew we would never die," seem a fitting statement at this time.

---

*In the spring of 2000, I returned a fourth time to meet some of the islanders who saved my life. The epilogue contains an account of this visit.

Regardless, they were men on whom our country could count and I will always be grateful and proud that I had the chance to serve with them.

PART THREE

FULL CIRCLE FOR A CACTUS AIR FORCE FIGHTER PILOT

The clear blue sky, where so many furious air battles were joined, is now at peace.

Walter Lord
Lonely Vigil: Coastwatchers of the Solomons

Chapter 28

Passing the Torch

I have two sons in the Navy Reserve, Lieutenant (jg) Michael DeBlanc (I.R.R.) [Inactive Readiness Reserve] and Petty Officer Richard DeBlanc (U.S.N.R.).*

In August 1972, only six months before the Vietnam cease-fire agreement, Seaman Richard DeBlanc arrived on Yankee Station in the Gulf of Tonkin on board the U.S.S. *Brooke* (DEG-1). The *Brooke* was one of the escorts of the aircraft carrier *Midway.* She arrived just in time to take part, along with other American warships, in the shelling of Haiphong Harbor in North Vietnam.

However, for some undetermined reason (to the crew's disappointment), the *Brooke* never got to join in the naval bombardment. Thus she was never fired at, which is the requirement for the combat decoration *V* for valor on certain military medals. The *Brooke*'s executive officer, Lieutenant Commander Boorda, would subsequently wear this decoration. Twenty-four years later, media inquiries about this apparently triggered the well-publicized suicide of Chief of Naval Operations (CNO) Admiral Mike Boorda!

---

*Except for the first paragraph and the last paragraph, this chapter was written by my son Richard. Over the years, he ascended from Seaman Recruit to Petty Officer First Class (E-1 through E-6). For the sake of simplicity, we will use the generic terms Seaman and Petty Officer in references to him.

From December 18 through December 29, 1972, Operation *Linebacker II* was launched with intensive bombing of North Vietnam, including heavy B-52 operations. Minefields in Haiphong Harbor and elsewhere were restocked. At night, Seaman DeBlanc, on his ship off the coast, would gaze at the explosions so bright that the clouds would shine.

On December 25, the thirty-six-hour Christmas bombing pause began. The North Vietnamese used this time to replenish their ammunition and supplies. More SAMs were brought forward. On December 30, President Richard M. Nixon ordered another bombing halt as the North Vietnamese showed interest in bargaining again.

On January 14, 1973, Seaman DeBlanc witnessed the last plane shot down in Vietnam. On January 12, Officers Kovaleski and Wise of VF-161 off the carrier *Midway* scored the last aerial kill of the war, the sixty-first for the carrier aircraft.* Ironically, two days later, their plane was hit by ground fire and they had to eject over the ocean. DeBlanc watched the two parachutes descend and shortly thereafter a helicopter arrived to pick up the men.

On January 27, 1973, a ceasefire agreement was signed in Paris, applicable to North and South Vietnam, but the *Brooke* remained off the coast until May of 1973. South Vietnam fell in April of 1975.

In January of 1976, Petty Officer DeBlanc left the Navy but returned in 1985 to the Navy Reserve when President Ronald W. Reagan's military buildup was in progress. The Cold War was still going strong, but then Mikhail Gorbachev came to power in the Soviet Union. The situation began to thaw. In 1990, the Cold War was officially over.

---

*Vic Kovaleski was an electrical engineer. He went on to serve twenty years in the service, winding up ferrying F-14s to Iran.

On July 31, 1990, the Soviet ships *Admiral Vinogradov* (DDG-554) and *Boyevoy (DDG-770)* and the oiler *Argyun* arrived at the Naval Station in San Diego, California. The scene on Pier Two there evoked images of the historic 1945 meeting of American and Soviet military forces at the Elbe River, signifying the Allied defeat of Nazi Germany. This time, sailors of the United States and Soviet navies exchanged handshakes to celebrate the armistice of the Cold War. Although virtually none of the Americans there that day had ever met a Soviet citizen before (and the same for the Russian sailors vis-à-vis Americans), there was no lack of communication. The obvious language barrier did not prevent plenty of bantering and clowning around—the universal language of young people. A friendly exchange unfolded between men of opposite front lines of the remaining "Cold War." It was hard to picture them ever engaging in a shooting war against each other. They seemed to have far more *in common* than *in conflict* as they posed like bosom classmates for photos.

One photo taken on board the *Admiral Vinogradov* displays U.S. sailors posing beside and inside a Soviet Helix helicopter, recognizable by its unique dual, overhead counter-rotating blades and no tail rotor. Helix helicopters were portrayed in Tom Clancy's novels (*The Hunt for Red October, Red Star Rising,* etc.).

Petty Officer DeBlanc, coincidentally, was in San Diego for his two weeks of active duty and was allowed to come aboard the Soviet ship. As he walked the gangplank and shook hands, he thought back to the years of the Cold War and was truly amazed that it was finally over. After centuries of fighting, mankind was closer to world harmony than ever before!

Both of my sons were on standby for possible deployment in Operation *Desert Storm* against Iraq until the situation was resolved. Michael is inactive now but was the past commanding officer of a Naval Mobile Construction Battalion unit (NMCB-28; CB = the SeaBees). Richard later transferred to Michael's old unit and remains in the reserves, ready to leave on a moment's notice in order to serve.

Chapter 29

The *Toa Maru* Connection

Events during the latter part of 1989 began to bring back memories of World War II. It began with a phone call from Lieutenant Colonel W. A. Beebe, officer-in-charge of Museum Branch activities, United States Marine Corps, Quantico, Virginia. I had just reached for my tennis racquet and was on the way out to play a few sets with friends when the phone rang. After the usual protocol, Lieutenant Colonel Beebe mentioned something about the sinking of a Japanese freighter, the *Toa Maru*, in Vella Gulf near Kolombangara Island, during an airstrike on the afternoon of January 31, 1943, in the Solomon Islands campaign. That caught my attention. Putting aside my tennis racquet, I listened carefully.

Lieutenant Colonel Beebe went on to say that Dr. Charles Darby of New Zealand was doing research on the sinking of the *Toa Maru* and wanted information about the four Marine fighter pilots who strafed the ship, causing it to sink. At this point, I quickly informed the lieutenant colonel that six Wildcat pilots had escorted twelve dive bombers up the Slot on the afternoon of January 31. The dive bombers missed the targets, however. Out of frustration, Lieutenant James L. Secrest and the other fighter pilots decided to strafe the ship. It was a quick decision on his part. Two Wildcats remained on high cover while Secrest and Lieutenant Joe Lynch began strafing runs. I didn't want to drop down to the water level because of my concern that we would be hit by Zeros. Near the water was certainly not the place to be in such a situation. But when the gun crew on the afterdeck of the Japanese freighter opened up with AA fire directed at Staff Sergeant Feliton (my wingman) and me, we decided to follow Secrest and Lynch down for one pass in order to silence the AA fire. By the time the Zeros came, Secrest was out of ammo and Lynch had a few rounds left. I did not know the name of the cargo ship we attacked on the last afternoon of January 1943.

Beebe was persistent. Dr. Darby had researched the Japanese records, which showed that after the Marine dive bombers had placed near hits around the ship, four fighter pilots in Wildcats (F4F-3s) strafed the ship, causing extensive fire damage in the main cargo area. The ship had to be scuttled on the reefs of Ghizo Island. If this were true, I responded, then Secrest and Lynch were the ones who did the damage since Feliton and I had simply made one strafing run on the gun platform located on the afterdeck of the cargo ship.

Beebe asked permission to pass along my address, phone number, and other pieces of information he had in his office to Dr. Darby. I said yes, knowing that future correspondence with Dr. Darby would show that I was not involved. After all these years, I thought that I had laid to rest my war experiences. Now it appeared that other events were beginning to surface, stirring up old memories again. I knew of Dr. Darby, keeping up with his research of the Yamamoto affair. I personally knew Major John Mitchell, Tom Lamphier, Rex Barber, and Raymond Hines from the last tour of duty we had on the 'Canal. Their successful interception of Admiral Yamamoto's

Betty bomber off Bougainville Island in the Solomons in April of 1943 was, as we have seen, a fantastic piece of flying and navigation during these early days of the war. It resulted in the death of Admiral Yamamoto, who had planned the Pearl Harbor strike.

Needless to say, my tennis matches that afternoon resulted in the loss of three straight sets. A few weeks later, I received a letter from Dr. Charles Darby, who gave me details of his research on the *Toa Maru*. His letter mentioned Peter Woodbury, a professional underwater photographer, and Danny Kennedy, a scuba diver and craft-shop owner who lives with his wife on Ghizo Island. The letter was the catalyst of a chain of events that I will narrate in these closing chapters. Woodbury and Kennedy would soon come to Louisiana and be the guests of Louise and me.

Peter Woodbury in Australia called me, requesting information on the mission against the *Toa Maru*. By this time I began to think that we really had been involved in the sinking of this ship. But I wanted no credit. I gave Peter the same response I gave Dr. Darby in my return letter to him. However, Peter was insistent. So I sent him materials and copies of my flight log book to verify the mission. After a series of phone calls and letters, Peter said that he planned to come in 1993 to the United States to attend a friend's wedding in Chicago. He wanted to drop by the Cajun country to visit. So began for me the saga of the *Toa Maru*.

The summer of 1993 finally arrived and Peter Woodbury, true to his word, arrived in the States. While still in Australia, he had asked about bus connections between Orange, Texas, and St. Martinville, Louisiana. His itinerary would include a stop in Orange to visit friends and another stop in Bowling Green, Kentucky, to interview a college professor who had been on Ghizo during World War II. I told him not to worry about transportation as I would go to pick him up in Orange. We would have hours of driving time, during which we could touch base on the information he was seeking.

The phone call from Peter came. The 200-mile trip to Orange was easy. More difficult was getting to the address where he was staying. He probably had as much trouble giving me directions as I had receiving it from him because of his Australian accent and my Cajun accent. I didn't get the correct names of his friends, though I did take down their phone number. After two wrong turns, I finally remembered the directions he gave and pulled up in the driveway of his friends' home. My mental picture of Peter and his friends led me to the expectation of meeting older men. As usual, I was wrong. They were between thirty and forty years old.

His friend's father had been in the SeaBees during World War II and had brought back memorabilia from Ghizo and Munda. I was fascinated by the professionalism of Peter's research and the items he showed me. We had a good visit, after which we drove to St. Martinville. During the trip, we discussed details of our flight's action on the *Toa Maru*. Peter had all the questions and I supplied the answers as best as I could. I know that war stories get better as we grow older, but I tried to give the facts as best as I could remember them, not from the "Monday morning quarterback" point of view. I could see that Peter had the *savoir-faire* for research.

Peter spent the night at a quaint bed and breakfast some two hundred feet from the famous Evangeline Oak in the heart of St. Martinville. Our town is one of the oldest in Louisiana and rich in culture. Peter stayed with Louise and me the next day. We drove him around Cajun country. In the den of my home, Peter and I sat down for an interview. I showed him the nine-foot spear I had taken from a native islander on Kolombangara in 1943. He was impressed with the flying fox wing bones and teeth placed neatly in pitch on the tip of the spear. The flying fox is a fruit bat found all over the Solomon Islands. I marveled at how Peter set up his photographic equipment, which fitted compactly in his backpack. He took many pictures, including one of my Medal of Honor.

As Peter was operating on a tight schedule, we left for New Orleans. On the way, he got to see some Louisiana sights, including the sixteen-mile-long I-10 causeway over the pristine Atchafalaya Basin, the mile-wide Mississippi River in Baton Rouge, and the state capitol building. We made a quick "coffee" stop at McDonald's before going to New Orleans International Airport (Moisant Field), where he confirmed his flight to Bowling Green, Kentucky. We parted company in the French Quarter. In March of 1994, I would receive some feedback and more questions from Peter.

Danny Kennedy took me by surprise one morning with a phone call from Florida. He and his wife ran a museum and scuba-diving place on Ghizo Island. His father was an airline pilot flying the Pacific route between the United States and Australia. In this connection, he had become interested in the Solomon Islands. While on a visit to the United States to get things for his business on Ghizo Island, he called me. Time and his itinerary would not permit a stop in St. Martinville, but he asked if I could come to see him in New Orleans. I was again a victim of the Aussie accent. I correctly understood the name of one of the hotels on St. Charles Avenue, near Tulane and Loyola universities. But I blew the phone number by one digit. Regardless, I had attended Loyola in 1949 and was familiar with New Orleans.

While I went to the Solomons in August of 1992 for the

fiftieth anniversary of the Battle of Guadalcanal, I did not attend the fiftieth anniversary of the sinking of the *Toa Maru* on January 31, 1993. With this in mind and with the fact that three other Cactus Air Force pilots and I had flown over Ghizo on August 10, 1992, for a "last strike against the Japanese," I felt an obligation to meet with Danny to clear up details while also getting a comprehensive picture of his setup on Ghizo. This time I would have all the questions. Finally the day arrived and I was on my way to New Orleans. The trip was nostalgic for me. Danny said that Ghizo was one of the most sought-after dive sites in the world because of the *Toa Maru* and the clear waters there. I was anxious to help, knowing that this was a source of income for the islanders who had saved my life during the war. I was in their debt.

Pulling into Loyola University to get my bearings and to use the phone, I noted the error in the number, got the correct one, and phoned Danny's hotel. He had left a message for me to wait in the hotel lobby for him. Driving down St. Charles Avenue, I saw the usual traffic and two streetcars, reminding me of college days. The clerk at the hotel set aside a portion of the lobby for the interview.

I selected a place where I could see the many guests entering and leaving, hoping to spot Danny as he entered. As usual, I was wrong. In came a young fellow who spotted my position, came up, and introduced himself as Danny Kennedy. We drank good New Orleans coffee and compared notes about Ghizo Island. We had our pictures taken together. The interview was taped. Danny is a professional and knows his business. I was amazed at the ease with which this young man handled his business and travel. He had complete confidence. As his schedule was tight, we soon finished and parted company. He said that he hoped that he and his wife could visit with Louise and me in St. Martinville on one of their trips to the States. He also gave me a current map of the Solomons and pointed out that the name "Kolombangara" was misspelled.

Later that year, our squadron had a reunion in Pensacola, Florida. It was good to bring up these events to the pilots who were involved in the sinking of the *Toa Maru*. Of the six fighter pilots who took part, two were still living, Jack Maas and me.

Chapter 30

Return to the Solomons (1992)

The month of July 1992 was one devoted to cutting grass. I was at our camp in Coteau Holmes doing my thing with the mini tractor and looking forward to returning to our home in St. Martinville in order to escape the heat. After three hours, I loaded the tractor in my Ford pickup and headed home. Little did I know that within the next hour and a half I would receive a call from Hawaii setting in motion a trip I had only dreamed about since the end of World War II.

After securing the grass-cutting gear, I hit the shower, dressed, and sat down in my favorite rocker to watch the local news on television. The phone rang and I picked it up to hear the voice of Lieutenant Colonel R. E. Stokes, U.S. Marine Corps Public Affairs Officer in Hawaii. My attention grew as he asked if I were interested in going to Guadalcanal to attend the fiftieth anniversary celebration commemorating the landing of the Marines there on August 7, 1942. He said that details were not yet finalized, but he felt confident that they soon would be. He was trying to get Medal of Honor pilots who were members of the Cactus Air Force to participate in the ceremonies on Henderson Field. It was a tentative plan on his part that had to be coordinated, after the higher-ups gave their approval, with passage aboard a Marine C-9 out of Andrews Air Force Base,

Maryland. Since we would be traveling with many other civilians, including journalists, we would have to pay for our meals and quarters. Of course, we would also pay for our airline passage from our hometowns to Andrews Air Force Base or to MCAS El Toro, California. Further expenses would be absorbed by us, including stopovers in Hawaii and four nights of hotel accommodations on Guadalcanal. The latter accommodations would be handled by a private organization, with details forthcoming.

This information sounded too good to be true. I hardly heard a word he was saying. My replies were yes, yes, yes, yes, regardless of the cost. He sensed my excitement and quickly informed me that there were a few strings attached, which he would clarify in a follow-up letter. With this and the usual protocol, Lieutenant Colonel Stokes concluded the phone conversation. I sat there for a few minutes, trying to gather my thoughts. Then I realized that nothing had been said about the wives. But I knew that this matter would be resolved one way or another.

Within a few days I received the long-awaited letter from Lieutenant Colonel Stokes. It had all of the flair of military correspondence that I remembered from my service days. "On behalf of the Commanding General of Fleet Marine Force, Pacific, Lieutenant General H. C. Stackpole III, it is my honor to confirm your flight aboard the military C-9 aircraft bound for Guadalcanal, to participate in the activities commemorating the 50th Anniversary of the battle for Guadalcanal." It went on to say that "although air transportation is provided at no cost, it will, however, be necessary for visitors to defray personal expenses for food and housing, etc. Valor Tours, Ltd. [Sausalito, California] requires advanced payment in the form of your check. . . . You will be assigned double occupancy with Brigadier General Robert E. Galer due to limited billeting accommodations in the Solomon Islands." The lieutenant colonel went on to say that I had the option to board the flight in Maryland or in El Toro, but I would have to pay for my transportation to and from either of those destinations.

Housing arrangements for my stay on Oahu, Hawaii, would be government quarters at minimum cost to me. Ground transportation to and from quarters would be provided. Naturally I would have to pay my airfare to and from Andrews Air Force Base, near Washington, D.C. I considered these minor details and would have gladly paid my way completely for this opportunity to return to the Solomon Islands. The usual protocol outlining details of medical and clothing requirements was included. One final note reflected passport requirements. Visas would be provided. The detailed itinerary followed.

Letters followed letters and there were many phone calls before all the details were worked out. I inquired about the part wives were to play in the scenario. I was told that wives could fly commercial airlines and that, although quarters on Guadalcanal were limited, they were available. This would be left up to us. I mentioned this to Louise and we started to make plans for her to come until I received another letter stating that the necessary shots and medical precautions had to be observed. These medical precautions and the memory of five years abroad in Europe were too much for her. We had recently been to Hawaii, so she decided not to make the trip.

I selected Andrews Air Force Base rather than El Toro as the place where I would board the C-9. It was a wise choice for me in terms of the return trip. Needless to say, I locked in all of the details of my flight and gave the fees necessary to complete the trip to Guadalcanal. It was now "hurry up and wait."

July 29, 1992, brought back memories. It was the day on which I purchased a round-trip airline ticket to Washington, D.C., with Continental Airlines. This was also the date back in 1941 on which I became a Seaman Second Class in the U.S. Navy for the flight-training program at the elimination base in New Orleans. It was the beginning of my flying career as a Naval, soon-to-be Marine, aviator. Now, the purchase of an airline ticket on this date set in motion my return to the Solomon Islands.

The day finally arrived. I had all the necessary immunizations. My passport was up to date and I had obtained the required visas. On August 2, 1992, I kissed my wife goodbye, drove the fourteen miles to Lafayette airport, parked my car in the long-term parking area, and boarded my flight to Washington National Airport,* Washington, D.C. I was on my way! The wife and I had visited our nation's capital many times, so I wasn't interested in what went on around Washington National when we landed and deplaned. I simply caught a cab for Andrews Air Force Base, where I arrived late on that afternoon. Departure for Hawaii would be the following day.

I had plenty of time to get billeted and look around. One never forgets military bases, so it was with little difficulty that I settled down. I found the officers' lounge and pool, signed in, and relaxed on the patio near the pool. After a good meal and drinks, I headed for my assigned quarters and turned in for a good night's sleep. I was scheduled to board the C-9 at 4:00 AM (0400 hours) on August 3. After setting my alarm and requesting an early wakeup call for 3:15 AM, I hit the sack. You guessed it, I was too excited to really get a good sleep. How could this

*Today, Ronald W. Reagan National Airport.

be possible with all of my past experiences? Well, I watched the clock from 1:00 AM through 3:15 AM, while I dozed on and off.

The alarm rang and I got my wakeup call. Packing was already done since I was used to making overseas flights to Europe during my five-year teaching tenure in the Netherlands. A car was waiting for me as I checked out of my assigned quarters. With a large cup of coffee in hand, I hopped into the car and headed for the C-9 at the terminal. Things hadn't changed much since the forties. It was the usual "hurry up and wait."

We were ready to taxi out on time when word was received that more journalists were coming on this flight to cover the ceremonies. Among these was Thomas B. Mechling of the *Washington Watch*. It was thirty minutes later that the C-9 took off, heading for MCAS El Toro, California. I slept most of the way and did not get a chance to meet most of my fellow passengers. There would be plenty of time later for this interaction.

Thirty minutes out of El Toro, the C-9 developed trouble with one of its VHF receivers, requiring a detour to San Diego for repairs. But before any flight changes were made, we received word that the necessary parts for the repair of this backup equipment were in El Toro, so we landed there on schedule. The rest of our fellow travelers were there, including Bob Galer, Jim Swett, and Ken Walsh. We were all Medal of Honor recipients, air aces, and members of the "Cactus Air Force," a title referring to combat pilots who fought on Guadalcanal against the Japanese in 1942 and in 1943. There were Navy pilots, Army pilots, Australian pilots, and New Zealand pilots fighting with us on the 'Canal in those days, though the greater part of the air action was borne by the Marines who flew Wildcats. The U.S. Army used P-38s, P-39s, and P-400s. A P-400 is the same as a P-39, but with a much larger tail and a 37mm cannon, instead of a 20mm cannon, synced through the propeller hub. New Zealanders used P-40s. P-39s, P-40s, and P-400s could not reach the altitude necessary to fight Japanese Zeros and Betty bombers. Hence, their function was mostly to strafe and fight against Japanese aircraft that ventured below 15,000 feet.

It was great seeing these old friends again. Jim Swett had the foresight to bring along a camcorder. He would be our cameraman for the trip. During the delay at El Toro, we also got in touch by phone with World War II pilots who were living in California.

By 4:00 PM (1600 hours), we were on our way to Hawaii. As usual, we were a few hours late, but we were outracing the sun and would make up the lost time. Jim Swett remarked that the plane was noisy and that we were as usual late in taking off (four hours, in fact). We had a few laughs and knew that the trip had started on a good note of camaraderie, since this was traditional terminology!

The five-hour flight passed quickly as we had the chance to meet our fellow passengers. They were journalists, Navy personnel, Marine ground troops, flight surgeons, and Navy nurses. They were all so young. Or were we too old? Regardless, we were all young at heart and in good health.

Dusk was settling in when we rounded Diamond Head, flew over the *Arizona* memorial, and landed at Hickham Field. Our quarters at Hickham were on the submarine base. There were single rooms for all, equipped with contemporary conveniences. You name it, they had it! It was like being on "Cloud 9." In the evening we relaxed at the Officers' Club instead of going downtown, given our full day of travel.

The next day was a day of rest as the C-9 was being prepared for the flight to Guadalcanal via Kwajalein Atoll. We were up early on the morning of the fourth, raring to get into downtown

Honolulu. The four of us hired a taxi and left the base to explore again the sights of Hawaii and to touch base with past history. It was a great day for shopping. The sun was up and the breeze from Waikiki Beach had that refreshing morning smell. The shopping malls had changed a bit since Louise and I had been here in 1983. Many Japanese were on the streets. In fact, many of the shops were owned by Japanese. We visited the *Arizona* memorial, the tower, and other sites. We failed to find Trader Vic's place. There were at Trader Vic's forty-eight ledgers reflecting the then forty-eight states. We used to sign our names in the ledger for our home state. Gradually we made our way late that afternoon to the Royal Hawaiian Hotel on Waikiki Beach and secured a table for the evening meal and entertainment.

An Australian couple had a table next to ours. Naturally the conversation turned to Sydney since all of us had been there during 1942 to 1943. The places we mentioned to the couple seemed "foreign" to them. Changes had occurred during the past fifty years. This left us embarrassed to a degree. They were a young couple and our terminology reflecting Sydney really dated us. The only common denominator was the Coathanger, the bridge overlooking Sydney's harbor. Even the size of the currency had changed. Pound notes were dollar size and coins were small. I took a pound coin from our friends only after I insisted on paying for their next round of drinks. (Later I sent this same coin to John Keenan.) The night passed quickly and the music was superb. All good things must come to an end. After all, we were not the same twenty- and twenty-one-year-old fighter pilots who had visited the Royal Hawaiian in 1942 and 1943. At a very late hour, we returned to the base for the night. Little did we realize that the morrow would bring us military "fringe benefits" that we did not want.

We were up the next morning bright and early, looking forward to the trip to Kwajalein and Guadalcanal. It was August 5, but in the Solomons it was August 6. After a good breakfast, the four of us returned to our rooms to freshen up and pack when we found notes on our doors asking us to report to sick bay for shots. This was a surprise, as we had already received all the immunizations indicated in our letters. It turned out that shots were not necessary, but that a new strain of mosquito carrying potent microbes had emerged since the war. We were then and there given two pills of doxycycline and a prescription for one each day for the next thirty-five days, well beyond the scope of our visit. The medical staff was insistent: no pills, no Guadalcanal. We took them.

We then boarded the plane. While routine checks were made, we talked about the "red carpet" treatment given to us in Hawaii by Lieutenant General H. C. Stackpole III, Commanding General of the Fleet Marine Force, Pacific. Our names were on the VIP board as we entered the complex. The general's staff set up an appointment for us. We were honored to be received by him, knowing his busy schedule and the important mission under his command. Although we were on a running time schedule, the general kept our meeting relaxed and informal, running even beyond the appointed time. Such was the degree of relaxation of military protocol.

Our conversation about this was interrupted for departure proceedings and we buckled in. We were on our way. The ten-hour flight ahead of us would take us below the equator and across the International Date Line. We would lose a day. There was a five-hour flight to Kwajalein. I had reservations about covering such a distance with an aircraft having only two jet engines. Flights over water for many hours are usually in four-engined aircraft such as the 747s I would fly to Europe. This slight reservation evaporated after an hour. This fully loaded aircraft could fly with one engine in an emergency. It is axiomatic with jets that trouble (excluding Murphy's Law) usually will develop within the first hour of flight. After burning jet fuel for that length of time, the engines have stabilized and will normally run trouble free for the balance of the flight. Besides, we flew this route with single-engined propeller fighter aircraft during the war for over eight hours of actual stick time. This would be my first landing in Kwajalein since World War II.

My thoughts turned to the Marshall Islands as I plowed through my brown-bag lunch. My second overseas combat tour began on the island of Engebi, an atoll on the rim of Eniwetok Atoll in the Marshalls. After World War II ended, these islands were used for nuclear tests. Was Kwajalein part of this research? Could the beaches still be radioactive, even at a low level? But these fears proved groundless.

Kwajalein was under the U.S. Army. We deplaned and had a chance to make a P.X. run for last-minute items we knew were not available on the 'Canal. During the break, I obtained a jeep and driver for a quick run down to the beach to obtain a sample of sand for the project I was completing for the coming reunion of VMF-112 in New Orleans that October. I would pick up the other samples of sand on the beaches of Guadalcanal and Wake Island.

During this stop, one of our passengers, Staff Sergeant Carmelo "Carlo" Cusmano from Florida, suffered a setback with a heart condition he had. The Navy Flight Surgeon aboard decided to return him to Pearl Harbor as there were top medical facilities available there. One of the doctors accompanied

Carlo aboard an Army tanker that had landed on Kwajalein on its way from Okinawa to Hawaii. We would miss him since he was part of the team and had a part in the ceremonies in Guadalcanal. Carlo is retired and has an interesting hobby. He collects sharks' teeth and makes earrings out of them. He is a good craftsman and gave us all a set of these earrings for our loved ones. Although we were sorry to see him depart, I sent him a VCR tape of the Solomon tour. I also ordered three sets of earrings for my granddaughters. Having bid Carlo farewell, we were soon on our way to the 'Canal.

The time was 3:00 PM (1500 hours) Guadalcanal time on August 6, 1992. What happened to the fifth of August, which started only a few hours before? Our plane was approaching the Florida Islands. Jim Swett cranked up his video camcorder and headed for the cockpit of the C-9, followed by Bob Galer, Ken Walsh, and me. We couldn't all crowd in, but we made certain that Jim was in a position to take pictures. Like first-time tourists, we were glued to the windows of the aircraft.

I cannot relate my thoughts and feelings as we approached the Florida Islands. In a flash, I had zeroed in on Tulagi, Savo, and Guadalcanal. Fifty years faded away for me and I am sure for my fellow aviators. We had been excited about at last reaching the islands, but we were each lost in our thoughts as we viewed the past presented to us after so many years. The island of Tulagi was in the "same place" but noticeably more inhabited. A quick glance across Iron Bottom Sound to Guadalcanal from our height revealed Henderson Field. But something wasn't right. I had flown many missions from this field during the war. The vegetation along the coast was almost gone. Honiara was spread over the coastal beach around Point Cruz. This used to be covered with coconut trees. Where were the cow pasture

(Fighter One) and Fighter Two? I started to question the others, but Jim Swett was too busy taking shots of Tulagi. He had become excited when he spotted Tulagi. This was the area where he shot down, in one fight, seven Japanese dive bombers before being shot down himself.

We were told to strap in for the landing. I couldn't take my eyes off the approach to the long single concrete runway stretched over the land and the lone high tower I remembered fifty years ago. The runway angle was wrong. That I sensed right away. I had made too many "carrier approaches" to this field to avoid pulling too wide in my approach, which would have invited enemy fire.

The landing was over and we were taxiing to the lone low terminal of Henderson Airfield. We deplaned to the tune of "Waltzing Mathilda" followed by the "Marine Corps Hymn," played by the Marine Corps Band near the hangar. We stood in awe of our surroundings, slowly drinking in the scenery. A few native islander young women presented each of us with a lei. Our party then drifted to the terminal to meet other island dignitaries and to check in with customs. We quickly dispensed with these. On a brass plaque inside the terminal were our names with the indication that we were aviators and recipients of the Medal of Honor.

As the plane bearing the generals was landing, we became part of the receiving line to welcome them. First off the aircraft was the Assistant Commandant of the Marine Corps, General John R. Dailey, and his wife. They were followed by Brigadier General Edwin Simms, Major General Charles E. Wilhelm, and others. This was a historic moment for us. We were honored to be a part of this golden anniversary. Before leaving Henderson Field for the Mendana Hotel (named after the Spanish explorer

Alvaro de Mendana) in downtown Honiara, some of the guys surprised the islander girls with a reciprocal action of placing leis over their heads, but with an added kiss on the cheek.

I was not surprised that our vehicle of transportation was Japanese made nor that we traveled on the left side of the road on the way to the Mendana. I was also trying my best to gather in the sounds, smells, vegetation, and orientation as we moved along. I was the first to be bitten by a mosquito that had ventured into our bus. As I swatted it, I remarked that this bite was due to my domicile near the swamps of Louisiana and was certainly not a reprisal from this mosquito, whose ancestors I had undoubtedly killed back in 1942. It brought a few laughs.

Departing for the Honiara Mendana Hotel, we crossed the Lunga River, which brought back old memories. Trying to identify the landmarks of 1942, I began to recognize Fighter Two, adjacent to the bay, as we approached Lunga Point. The former runway was now completely covered with warehouses. To the left of the runway, in the area where we taxied our fighters after landing on Fighter Two, was a golf course. Only the east end of the runway was discernible since it was an approach to the tall coconut trees bordering the Lunga River. We continued on to the Matanikau River. This brought back memories of the ill-fated Goettge Patrol. If only they had landed *beyond* Point Cruz!

We quickly occupied our assigned rooms. Tired from the flight and suffering from jet lag, we nevertheless managed, in the usual Marine aviators' manner, to trot down to the patio near the beach for relaxation and a few drinks. The Mendana would be our home base for the next four days. (We were scheduled to leave on August 10.) Jim Swett had us retrace our entrance steps for the benefit of his camcorder, beginning with Brigadier General Bob Galer and ending with Ken Walsh. But

I quickly pointed out to Jim that he would not be in the picture unless I operated the camera. With a drink in his hand and a grin on his face, I filmed him coming around the corner of the open lobby amid the laughter and comments of the group around the table.

Day one was drawing to a close, but much remained to be done. There was just enough time to get a few drinks under our belt when we were given the schedule for that evening's events. At 6:00 PM (1800 hours), a reception would be hosted by His Excellency, Sir George Dennis Lepping, G.C.M.G., M.B.E., K. St. J., Governor General of the Solomon Islands, and Lady Lepping at the State House, East Kola'a Ridge. This would be followed by a reception hosted by U.S. Ambassador Robert W. Farrand, Captain Robert B. James, U.S.N., and Major General R. H. Barrow, U.S.M.C., aboard the U.S.S. *Racine* (LST-1191). Thayer Soule would later present at the Mendana a screening of rare footage filmed on Guadalcanal in 1942 and 1943. What a pace to follow after a ten-hour flight following little sleep from the night out on the town, crossing the International Date Line with the loss of a full day, and a few moments to get room assignments and to relax.

We quickly returned to our rooms and prepared for the evening's events. I suggested to Bob Galer that we wear our Medals of Honor for the events, since I had seen the islanders wearing their wartime decorations. He agreed and word was passed to Ken and Jim. Bob and I shared room 416 while Jim and Ken shared room 414. There was a beautiful view of the beach, Iron Bottom Sound, Lunga Point, and Savo Island.

Honiara is a coastal town. Night was rising (or falling) quickly on Guadalcanal and I could identify with this. The moon was down. The streetlights were yellow, with low-wattage bulbs. As the electrical circuits are 220 volts and 50 cycles, I mentioned to Jim that he would have trouble using his electric razor unless he brought along an adaptor transformer to obtain 120 volts and 60 cycles.

Emotions began to flare up in me after attending the initial island protocol ceremonies with the Governor General. The boat trip to the U.S.S. *Racine* was in total darkness except for the sea navigational lights. As we boarded at Point Cruz Wharf the craft that would take us to the ship, I had this strange, overwhelming feeling that carried me back in time over fifty years when I shot down two Japanese Betty bombers near this very spot and smoked a third. From an altitude of fifty feet, they were attacking our fleet anchored nearby. I shook this feeling quickly as we approached the *Racine*. However, memories began again as a speeding craft passed our starboard side, leaving a phosphorous wake. On January 29, 1943 (4:00 AM or 0400 hours), during dawn patrol, my Wildcat engine failed while I was flying on instruments, as we awaited an expected Japanese attack at daybreak. The wake of the U.S.S. *Jenkins* lit up the bay, enabling me to safely make a deadstick landing right about where the *Racine* was anchored this very evening. I was glad that the dark night hid my emotional state before boarding the ship.

I had the pleasure of meeting many officers and men from Louisiana. Some had attended L.S.U., the university from which I obtained two of my degrees. We had an enjoyable evening and were given the VIP treatment. I sometimes feel that war stories get better with age and in an environment far away from danger. But I don't believe that we were guilty of any drifting away from actual details when we were questioned by the journalists aboard. I told a reporter from New York about shooting the bombers near the site where he was interviewing me. My remarks were printed in the *New York Times* and sent to me later by a friend. The reporter even mentioned that, during the interview, I was grasping the Medal of Honor about my neck! We extended the usual Navy protocol to the captain of the *Racine* and took our leave for the evening. This ship had embarked from the United States, a month in advance, with troops from the 1st Marine Division out of Camp Pendleton, California. (The 1942 landings on Red Beach, Guadalcanal, were done by the 1st Marine Division.) After a stop in Sydney, Australia, these young Marines prepared the way for us by building camp lodgings for the coming ceremonies. We returned to the hotel. Tomorrow, August 7, D-Day in the Solomons in 1942, would be a busy day.

Chapter 31

Fiftieth Anniversary

Friday, August 7, 1992, began with a bang. I'm sure that many of us wished to remain in the sack for a few more hours, but we were scheduled to go to as many events as possible, if we desired. Bob Galer suggested that we follow through and we did. A dawn service was held at 6:00 AM (0600 hours) at the Old Cenotaph War Memorial on Mendana Avenue. The site was within walking distance, just opposite our hotel. After the services, we took many pictures of the Cenotaph and surroundings. Returning to the hotel for breakfast and coffee, we met many Marine veterans who came with their wives and were quartered at the Mendana.

The dedication of the Guadalcanal Campaign Memorial on Skyline Ridge, followed by the laying of wreaths in memory of those who died during the Guadalcanal campaign, took most of the morning. We were furnished transportation to the site but had to abandon the small bus as the road was blocked with a large crowd of islanders and military personnel of different nationalities. It was nice to walk up there. Inscribed on the many beautiful altar stones are the names of all the organizations, ground and air, that took part in the campaign. I quickly found VMF-112 and happily pointed it out to the others as Jim Swett recorded it on tape. This action was repeated by the other aviators.

For the record, we would take part in the ceremonies on Henderson Field since we were all members of the Cactus Air Force. Bob Galer was commanding officer of VMF-224. He was the senior Cactus pilot in our group, having reached the fighting early in October 1942. I was next as I was a member of VMF-112 and reached the 'Canal in November 1942. Jim Swett (VMF-221) and Ken Walsh (VMF-124) followed in February 1943.

During the ceremony, I had the pleasure to meet Martin Clemens again, who was a coastwatcher on Guadalcanal during 1942. Little did I realize that this chance meeting would start a chain reaction leading to memories of my dealings with the coastwatchers after I was shot down on January 31, 1943. I mentioned to Martin that while I was teaching in Europe, I had the pleasure of visiting Henry Josselyn and his wife, Pat, at their home in Ipswich, England. Since Henry, one of the two coastwatchers responsible for my rescue, was now deceased, I expressed my condolences on the death of John Keenan, the other coastwatcher who was, I had heard, betrayed in 1943 by the natives on Bougainville Island. I was pleasantly surprised when Martin Clemens told me that John Keenan was alive and well and that he was in touch with him. Martin asked for my card and promised that he would forward John's address to me after he returned home. My reactions were that of the twenty-one-year-old pilot who fought in World War II. I couldn't believe what he was telling me. I was so sure that John had been betrayed and killed during the war. Little did I realize that the coming event at 3:15 PM (1515 hours), the unveiling of the Vouza statue and the dedication of the Solomon Islands Campaign Memorial, would match and even surpass the news of John Keenan's survival. All this in one day! How could these chains of events play such a leading role in closing "full circle" the events of my war experience?

Sir Jacob Vouza, whose statue was unveiled that afternoon at Police Headquarters, Rove, was a native islander and served under Martin Clemens during the dark days of Guadalcanal fighting. Had it not been for Vouza's loyalty to the Allied cause, I do not believe that we would have won the Solomons campaign. A Guadalcanal police officer, he was captured by the Japanese. Vouza refused to answer questions about the Americans. He suffered torture at the hands of the Japanese, almost beyond human endurance. Left for dead, Vouza chewed through the ropes that held him captive. Although shot three times and bayoneted, he survived and crawled to our lines. He gave valuable and current information to General Vandegrift on the disposition of Japanese forces. He survived the war, living well into his eighties.

The unveiling was completed in blisteringly hot tropical weather. Many of the young Marines, standing at rigid attention, passed out. Water was hurriedly given to them. Martin Clemens and others participated in the ceremonies before the unveiling. Clemens did the actual unveiling. It is a well-constructed statue. Jacob Vouza, machete in hand, is clothed in the loincloth (lavalava) of the forties. Many of the islanders unaccustomed to events of the past resented this form of dress for such a hero as Vouza, preferring the majestic garb in which he was vested when knighted by the Queen of England. Regardless, this didn't detract from the moving ceremonies. At the conclusion of the ceremony, Bob Galer, Jim Swett, Ken Walsh, and I laid a wreath.

During the ceremony, I spoke with the native representative from Kolombangara and Vella La Vella. He was dressed in a suit with lavalava and is a man about my age. I spoke with him about the period when I was shot down and rescued by men from his village. He didn't remember the incident. He did recall rescues of Allied pilots by the coastwatchers as well as rescues of Japanese pilots by their own forces.

Seeing many Marines from the line companies crying during the ceremonies left me with a feeling of guilt. They fought twenty-four hours a day and stayed with the dead all around them. I tried to rationalize my feelings about this. After taking off from the cow pasture, we fought in the air for a few brief moments at high speed. Then we landed. Throughout the campaign, we knew of course about the terrible action going on around us. We shared with the ground troops shelling from Japanese ships. When called by their company commanders, we strafed Japanese positions near them. But we did not have to live with the dead around us. Yet the loss of our friends was noted when we landed. There would be an empty bunk next to ours. Later, when flying up the Slot, I would come to grasp more fully the emotional trauma these men were undergoing.

During the unveiling, I met Father John Craddock. He was speaking with a few of the Americans near me. During a lull in the program, I joined in the conversation. He introduced himself as a Marist priest, serving as an officer with the New Zealand Navy for the unveiling. He was also at the time a teacher at St. Joseph Catholic School, located on the Tenaru River, at the site from which the Japanese would launch their assaults against Henderson Field during World War II. Naturally I wanted him to know that Louise and I have a son who is a Roman Catholic priest serving as pastor of Our Lady of Mercy Church in Henderson, Louisiana. We noted the parallel between Henderson Field and Henderson, Louisiana.*

*My son is currently pastor of Our Lady of Mercy Catholic Church in Opelousas, Louisiana. [2001 note]

Father Craddock told me that he would soon be visiting the U.S.A. on a fund drive and would like to visit us in St. Martinville. I told him that we would be delighted to have him. True to his word, he came to Louisiana that November and was a guest in our home. He celebrated Mass in our home church, St. Martin de Tours. He also concelebrated Mass with our son, Father Jeff DeBlanc, in Our Lady of Mercy Church, Henderson. I invited Father Craddock to the Mendana for an evening get-together with World War II aviators. He accepted my invitation and we had an excellent meal and conversation on the open-air portion of the Mendana complex.

The events culminated with a reception and cultural show, hosted by the Honiara Municipal Authority, at the Mendana Hotel's outdoor pavilion. Native dancers, surrounded by young Marines representing the 1st Division, were featured.

Saturday, August 8, day three, was a clear and beautiful day, though the heat was still with us. We prepared to attend the dedication of Edson's Bloody Ridge Memorial and the dedication of Henderson Tower Memorial at Henderson Airfield. As aviators flying off Henderson Field, we would present wreaths during the ceremonies. Ground personnel presented their portion of the program. Martin Clemens introduced the various speakers. General John Dailey, Assistant Commandant of the U.S. Marine Corps, spoke about the ordeals staging out of Henderson Field and the role we played. He mentioned each one of us and said that we were all fighter pilots, aces, and recipients of the Medal of Honor, flying off this very field in 1942 and 1943. A fifth Medal of Honor recipient of the Korean War, but one who previously fought on Guadalcanal during those days, was General Raymond G. Davis, U.S.M.C. (Ret.), who represented U.S. President George H. W. Bush. He commanded an anti-aircraft battalion on Guadalcanal. He spoke about the Americans and the Allies. Dr. E. Kaplan, M.D., was Master of Ceremonies. Also present on the platform were Major General Charles E. Wilhelm, Commanding General, 1st Marine Division. General Wilhelm and Major Martin Clemens unveiled the memorial. General Davis and General John Dailey cut the ribbon, officially opening the tower. As a unit, we laid the wreaths around the tower. The invocation, prayer, and benediction were given by Navy Commander Robert A. Black, Chaplain. From there we proceeded to the Henderson Terminal for the dedication of the Heroes' Wall, a monument to air personnel killed while trying to secure the airfield during the battle. The remainder of that Saturday, August 8, and the whole of Sunday, August 9, were ours.

It was at this time that I joined Major Bill Fisher of Covington, Tennessee. During the war, Bill was a sixteen-year-old ammo carrier for the 2nd Raider Battalion on Guadalcanal. I would hear from him soon after this tour. We were all pilots flying out of the cow pasture, Fighter One. Our associations with the island were the Slot and the airfield. I would personally become acquainted with the ground battle sites during my second visit in 1995 and third visit in 1996, when I would accompany Major Bill Fisher and John Innes, the latter an authority on the Guadalcanal campaign.

Sunday arrived and the mission we were sent on as Medal of Honor recipients was completed. I had made plans to spend time with Father Craddock after morning Mass. From the Mendana Hotel, I walked eight blocks to the Catholic church for the open-air Mass. A Bishop from New Guinea was the celebrant. The beautiful services and homily were enhanced by native chants and music. After Mass, Father Craddock took me to the school system. I really got a good overview of their educational system. The school was located on the site of the wartime Naval medical facilities, on the banks of the Tenaru River. Some of the medical Quonset huts still remained, but in rusty condition. The school personnel came from all over the Solomons. Dormitories similar to G.I. quarters were set up for housing students. However, there were no beds, only hammocks. I was impressed with some of the students' work on display. The quality and penmanship were outstanding! I vowed then and there to keep in touch with this school system via computer/fax modem.

During the tour, I was momentarily distracted by a beautiful bird that I hadn't seen in over fifty years. It is comparable in size to our mockingbird. I call it "Willie Wagtail," because it simply flies by, lands near you, and begins to wag its tail like a metronome keeping time with some tune. Father Craddock called it the fantailed warbler.

Like the parrot, the mockingbird is an "imitator," but to a lesser extent. It imitates the song notes of many other birds and other sounds—the barking of a dog, for instance! In the southern U.S., the mockingbird sings both day and night. What the nightingale is to Europe, the mockingbird is to the South. Returning to the Mendana, Father and I had another hour of lively conversation before we parted company.

Chapter 32

"Last Strike"

A pleasant surprise awaited me when I joined up with the other fellows. General Galer, true to his word, had arranged a "last strike against the Japanese," a flight up the Slot. We planned to leave after Sunday lunch. While we were still in Hawaii, I brought up the possibility of such a flight. This was documented on Jim Swett's videotape. We were all elated and thanked Bob for setting it up. We would board a Marine C-12 on the tarmac in Guadalcanal. The plane's pilots were here overnight on their way to Guam the next day. Bob had spoken with the powers that be, who let us use the plane that Sunday afternoon for our "strike." A Marine major would be our pilot, with a colonel as copilot.

I wanted to contact Louise to find out how things were at home. In a matter of seconds, I was on the phone and talking with her in St. Martinville. Later I checked the phone bill, which listed $18 for the call. This was not bad for an almost instant dial response from Guadalcanal. I was impressed, since I had also worked for ten years for Bell South Phone Company after retiring from AFCENT school system.

After lunch, we left the Mendana and went to Henderson Airfield. Having an hour to spare, we walked around the terminal looking for familiar landmarks that would help us locate

Fighter One and our tenting areas from the war. In the process, we discussed the visit we had with the airline pilots who flew the route between Guadalcanal and Sydney, Australia. We had been invited to the summer coastal cottage a few klicks from the center of Honiara. It was lovely and really cool for this part of the day.

There was another comparable cottage farther up the beach toward Honiara and we inquired as to its occupants. To our surprise, they said that it was empty. It appears that many occupied the cottage over the years, but they all left because they claimed it was haunted! The natives shy away from the place. Many have reported that ghosts of Japanese and American soldiers walk through the house at night. Well, that was a twist! Could this have been the site of the Goettge massacre? It was in the approximate location of the patrol's ambush. It would be nice to get to the bottom of these ghost stories if they are indeed true and not merely island folklore.

The C-12, a twin-engined prop jet, was ready for boarding. After the usual military protocol, we scrambled aboard like high-school kids. Jim Swett positioned himself to take video shots of the entire "mission." Take-off was always over the bay (north) and not the mountainous interior (south). First we circled Tulagi and Jim Swett pointed out the place where he was shot down the first time. Somehow the island looked different from the days I flew over it. Where was the place I saw Joe Palko crash after his collision with Pedersen? The island seemed larger.

The pilots banked the aircraft to a heading of about 300 degrees to pass over Savo Island and Cape Esperance on Guadalcanal's western tip. We were on our way over the Slot at an altitude of 1,500 feet. As usual the cloud cover was heavy, but visibility below our altitude was excellent. We all crowded around the flight deck. Our airspeed was 200 knots. We would fly over the Russell Islands located about sixty miles away. In less than half an hour, we had the islands in sight and looked at the old fighter strip. I had landed on the Russells a few times, but this was not the strip I remembered. As I recall, the strip was shorter and thick groves of coconut trees flanked the runway. Now the whole place was bereft of trees. Jim Swett and Ken Walsh remember the way it was since they used these facilities long after Bob Galer and I left the 'Canal.

The Russells were the location where Jim Percy was shot down. After he bailed out, his chute didn't fully deploy, causing him to fall 2,000 feet. But he survived! After my return to the States, I sent Jim Percy the complete VCR film. He could not get over how many more little islands were around the Russell Islands. They looked so large now! I agreed with him.

Our next set of islands up the Slot would be New Georgia, Kolombangara, and Vella La Vella. Segi Point was on New Georgia. The airfield there was not functional during my time on Guadalcanal as we struck Munda Field above this spot. We were now flying north of the group of islands. Jim Swett pointed out the location where he had been shot down the second time. In the meantime, he was capturing all this on video.

Bob Galer could not identify with this territory since his fighting had been confined mostly over and around Henderson Field. He was there during the dark days of defensive fighting. I too was part of this defensive action. But Bob left me on the 'Canal when our tactics shifted from the defensive to the offensive after January 1943.

We were now approaching the island of Kolombangara. It was between Kolombangara and Vella La Vella that I was shot down, beating President Jack Kennedy to the island by six months. I was glued to the window of the aircraft as we passed over Vila Field, the wartime Japanese field that held Zeros. The field was still there, but the runway was overgrown with vegetation. How I wished to go down there and walk around the island. I spotted the place where I landed in the ocean across the island from Vila Field and swam to shore so long ago. I desperately tried to recognize the place where I had come ashore after my six-hour swim. The circular island looked smaller, less dangerous, and the volcano in its center did not seem to be 5,000 feet high. I looked for the stream leading from the dormant volcano, partly hidden in the low overcast. It was not visible. I looked for the little hut I had slept in so long ago. No luck. The coast was smooth and still bare of civilization. There was very little rain forest. The trees seemed to have been thinned out. (I found out recently that a timber company worked the island for over twenty years.) Kolombangara seemed to have melted into the Pacific over these past fifty years.

Was it my age or had my youth (twenty-one years of age then) blinded my eyes and amplified the hidden terror I felt when I was shot down? This was deep in enemy territory as all Allied forces were still confined to the inner limits of Henderson Field. At that time, I had no knowledge of coastwatcher activities and assumed that everyone around there was hostile to Americans. We had been briefed about showing no fear if caught by the natives. We were told that there was enough intelligence information to verify that some local natives on these islands were for us, others against us. Survival this far up the chain could go either way. The Japanese offered an incentive bonus to the natives if they handed over American pilots. Thankfully, everything worked out in my favor. I continued to gaze at the view below, lost in my thoughts. It was only when we headed back around Kolombangara and passed over Munda Field (still there) that I became emotional over my trip to the Solomons. I could then identify with the emotions displayed earlier by the ground troops. I would no longer have a feeling of guilt. I located the places of seven of my nine aerial kills and could even mark it on the waves, creating on the ocean a "visible ground map" of the Munda area.

My attention swung to Ghizo Island and Vella La Vella. These seemed about the same. I could identify the route we took to the *Toa Maru* and Missionary Silvester's Bilou plantation. I also saw Plum Pudding Island, now named Kennedy Island, to which Jack Kennedy brought the survivors of *PT-109*.

Finally, we were past the 250-mile radius and headed back for Guadalcanal, taking the southerly route on an easterly heading. As mentioned, this part of the flight would take us over Munda Airfield, which was still a functional airport. As we flew over the runway, I could see the channel between Rendova Island and Munda Field. I located the spot where I shot down the float plane hanging on to Lieutenant Poole's dive bomber back in December 1942. As we left from over the field, Jim Swett began to hop from one window to another, filming away with his camera. Here was the spot where he was shot down the second time. Leaving New Georgia Island, we could see the Russell Islands in the distance. Navigation was a piece of cake for us during the war since the Slot was comparable to an interstate highway in the sky, so long as there was daylight and good weather.

We were all quiet for the return leg, which Jim Swett faithfully recorded on his camcorder. I tried to read the expressions of my fellow passengers, but to no avail. Their expressions did not betray their emotions. The trip back remained relatively quiet, with some small talk. We were emotionally drained. Upon landing on Henderson Field, we thanked our pilots, took addition-al pictures, and bid them farewell. We had come "full circle" on this last flight against the Japanese.

On Monday, August 10, there was time to make a quick trip during the morning to "Bonegi One" and "Bonegi Two," the sites of the two Japanese transport ships we had strafed in November 1942. The captains of these transports beached them to save the lives of as many Japanese troops as possible. As a young pilot, I had placed many a .50-caliber round of ammo into the hulls of these transports. Now the superstructure was down to the waterline, but in clear water. This site is now used as a scuba-diving haven for tourists. The cab that took us from the hotel to this site halted at the gate for us to pay the five-dol-lar entrance fee. But the islanders would not take our money, as the cab driver said that we were Marines returning for the anniversary ceremonies. With our group were Navy medical doctors and nurses who had come to scuba dive. No one may take souvenirs from these diving sites. The lapping of the tide against the shoreline registered with me. Branded forever in my mind were my nights spent alone on Kolombangara. The rest of the fellows were having a ball on the beach, taking pic-tures and running up and down. I was lost in my thoughts but soon rejoined them. We finally left the group and returned to the hotel. It was good to have visited this site.

We were now ready to check out of the hotel and head for Henderson Airfield to board the plane to Wake Island. An air-port tax of US $15 was required for exiting and we all exchanged our money for the tax. But the tax did not apply to us. Since we could not exchange the currency back to American dollars, we all donated the fee to David Vouza and his family in memory of his father, Jacob Vouza. This action on my part opened the doors for an appointment to the *ad hoc* committee raising money to bring David Vouza to the United States, giving him the VIP treatment we gave his father years ago. This opened further my association with personnel from the island, which I had not dreamed would happen. With the usual goodbye protocol over, we boarded the C-9. The crew taxied the plane to the runway and we were on our way. Before liftoff, I made certain that the sand samples I had taken from Red Beach, "Bonegi One," and "Bonegi Two" were in my possession. I would design a scaled map of this part of the globe and place sand particles from each island indicated. The entire 8" by 10" sheet would be laminated for presentation to the members of VMF-112 at our reunion later that year.

Jim Percy, a friend of mine and a member of VMF-112 in 1942, had mentioned that his brother was a civilian worker on Wake Island when it fell in 1942 to the Japanese. His brother survived the ordeal as a prisoner of war.

Wake Island would be our landing site for refueling before we crossed the International Date Line on the flight to Hawaii. Once we crossed the Date Line, it would be August 9 again. We visited the sites where the surrender to the Japanese took place and vice versa when we recaptured Wake Island. It was nice to see in peacetime all of the first-line fighter planes for defense of the island or deployment to the Far East. After a two-hour stay on the island, we took off for Hawaii. We stayed there overnight.

We took off early on the morning of the tenth as we would be losing daylight and could not outrace the sun. The rest of the trip was mundane, similar to the usual flights we had so often completed over the years. Hence, we simply sat back and slept the rest of the way. We arrived in Washington around 2:00 AM (0200 hours) on August 11. I took a flight to Lafayette,

Louisiana, at 6:00 AM (0600 hours) that same day.

The trip was very interesting. We played our part in the cere-monies, which were now part of history. But within a few months, I would be in contact with Bill Fisher, who facilitated two more trips to the Solomons (1995 and 1996). These would be person-ally rewarding trips that put me into contact with the coastwatch-er John Keenan, who I thought had been killed during the war, and with Ati, the native who saved my life on Kolombangara.

* * * *

It was great to be back home. Events began to arrive at a fast pace, including Hurricane Andrew, which came ashore in Louisiana with 140-mile-per-hour winds on Wednesday, August 26, 1992, two weeks after my return. The eye of the hurricane passed just to the east of St. Martinville. Cleaning up after the storm was quite a job. We were also without electricity for sev-eral days. Louise cooked our meals on the barbecue pit! Each morning, I would bring our electric coffee pot to the neighbor-ing Sheriff's Office, which had emergency power, so we could enjoy freshly brewed coffee.

Later that fall, as I mentioned, Father Craddock visited us, staying in our home on the weekend before Thanksgiving (Friday, November 20, through Sunday, November 22, 1992).

Chapter 33

Battle of Guadalcanal and Solomon Islands Foundation

I received letters from many of the friends I met while on the trip to the Solomons. Reading two letters in particular brought me upright in my chair. The first was from my Florida acquaintance who had a heart problem while we were on the way over to Guadalcanal. As mentioned earlier, he had an unusual hobby—gathering sharks' teeth and making earrings out of them. He gave me a pair for my daughter and I ordered others for my granddaughters. In return, I sent him VCR tapes of the trip and ceremonies that he had missed. It made his day.

The second letter, from Major Bill Fisher, would change my retirement days. Bill is from Covington, Tennessee, as I mentioned. During October 1942, he was a sixteen-year-old machine-gun ammo carrier for Carlson's Raiders, 2nd Battalion. Like many of us who returned to civilian life after the war, Bill had entered law school, from which he graduated. He was now interested in preserving battle sites on Guadalcanal for future generations, similar to the way Civil War sites are preserved here in the States, including Shiloh in his home state. He asked me to join his staff and represent informally the "air portion" of the association. Bill is a man of few words and lots of action. He was with us during the 1992 ceremonies and was not at all impressed with the upkeep of the battle-site markers. His expertise in law and journalism and his connections with an Australian computer businessman on Guadalcanal were factors he put to good use to launch the Battle of Guadalcanal and Solomon Islands Foundation. One of the purposes of the foundation is, in the words of the charter, "to promote through the encouragement of the study of the Battle of Guadalcanal and the Solomon Islands a deeper understanding of the role and sacrifices of the men of the armed forces of all participating nations and the natives of the Solomon Islands who shared in the hardships incurred." In addition, the foundation will promote the location, identification, development, and maintenance of "the battle sites and . . . provide for their preservation, perpetuation."

How could I refuse to join? Bill had put his life on the line twenty-four hours a day, while I as a pilot was not in such continuous jeopardy. Bill would represent the ground actions, while I would represent the air actions. This set in motion my second return trip to Guadalcanal. We would be quartered in the home of Mr. John Innes, affiliated with TechniSyst Computer Electronics, Honiara, Guadalcanal. John was an authority on the history of the Guadalcanal campaign. Bill hinted to me that we would have to make more than one trip back to the island. He told me, among other things, that the Japanese would not be opposed to changing the name of Henderson Field!

Bill had some Washington, D.C., connections. Lieutenant General Harold Blot was making a Pacific-rim trip from Washington to Hawaii, then to Australia, the Solomons, Iwo Jima, Okinawa, Korea, and Alaska, before returning to Washington, a trip of over 27,000 miles. Bill made arrangements to board the general's aircraft at Andrews Air Force Base, Maryland, and asked if I were interested in going along.

I quickly informed him that I already had my "track shoes" on! We met at the Bachelor Quarters, Andrews AFB, on October 19, 1995, and departed the next day from Andrews for Travis AFB in California. The general's plane was a beauty, a C-20 executive jet capable of carrying twenty passengers and flying at an altitude of 45,000 feet, well above the commercial jets, which flew below 38,000 feet. We were six in the aircraft, not counting the flight crew, as we proceeded to outrace the setting sun for Kaneohe Marine Corps Base, Hawaii, arriving late in the afternoon of the same day, the twentieth.

The two-day stay in Hawaii gave Bill and me a chance to look over the base and its facilities and to enjoy a little R & R at the Officers' Club. We were going to Guadalcanal to participate in a ceremony rededicating Henderson Field. We went over the details relative to the battle sites and maintenance thereof, which we would discuss with the governing body of Guadalcanal. We departed Kaneohe MCB on October 23 and arrived on Guadalcanal on October 24, crossing the International Date Line. Bill managed to get the general to agree to put us on the flight manifest for return to the States via the Pacific rim. (We had been scheduled to return to Hawaii on October 27.) John Innes met us at Henderson Field and brought us to his home in the Honiara hills. I shared a room with Colonel Joe Mueller, a Los Angeles policeman and Marine reservist. He is also an authority on the Goettge Patrol.

Marine Reserve General Frederick P. Henderson, brother of the dive-bomber Marine pilot (Major Lofton R. Henderson) killed during the Battle of Midway and for whom Guadalcanal's Henderson Field was named, would officiate at the rededication ceremony, which was probably the last such event. Several million dollars are being spent to bring the field up to date.

Ironically, the money is a gift from the Japanese. The United States gave the Parliament Building and the Japanese are covering the cost of the airfield. Regardless, the name Henderson will remain as the official name of the airfield on Guadalcanal. The Henderson family was most gracious in presenting the plaque. I also had the chance to renew acquaintances with Father John Craddock, who was kind enough to attend the functions, even cutting short two of his classes to be able to do so.

The next day we attended a meeting of the governmental body of Guadalcanal. Bill Fisher explained the reasons for forming the Battle of Guadalcanal and Solomon Islands Foundation. What triggered the project was Bill's second trip to the Solomons in 1992 and then the visit of David Vouza to the United States. David is the son of Sergeant Major Sir Jacob Vouza, who was so instrumental in helping the Marines during the battle for Guadalcanal. We obtained permission to carry on this idea of preserving battle sites on the island and were told that we would receive help from the local government to accomplish the goals of the foundation. After another day of rest, we left for Hawaii aboard the C-20. Then, we left Hawaii for Iwo Jima and Okinawa. We rejoined General Blot on Okinawa, where he was looking into the problems Marines were having vis-à-vis the civilian population. He would succeed in easing the tension between the Marines and the Okinawans. In the meantime, we were at Iwo Jima and, I might add, it brought back many memories of my youth and the battle we had there. The runway was neat and filled with Japanese jet fighters. I could not get adjusted to this situation. We entered the air terminal and noted a few of the Japanese fighter pilots hanging around the flight operations desk. We were soon airborne again and on our way to Korea after having refueled the

C-20. We played the role of tourists in Seoul. I visited the DOD school system for the students of American military personnel. It brought back memories of the five years we spent in Holland, where I taught the children of American dependents at AFCENT in Brunssum. I could also identify with the surroundings of Korea, where my brother, Maryknoll Brother Ralph (Frank) DeBlanc, spent thirty years as a missionary.

We took off for the Marine Corps Air Station in Iwakuni, Japan. Lieutenant General Blot had completed his mission on Okinawa, and after a day on Japanese soil, we left for Alaska. The flight to Anchorage was at night and the vista was very beautiful. We flew at 45,000 feet, above the weather. The earth appeared to curve on the horizon and the aurora borealis was gorgeous.

Our stay in Alaska was short and soon we were off on the final leg of our flight. We arrived at Andrews AFB, Maryland, at dawn on October 27. On the twenty-eighth, Bill and I took a flight to Memphis, where he left for Covington, Tennessee, and I for Lafayette, Louisiana, and home. It was a good flight.*

---

*The foundation so far has little money to carry out its goals but plans to raise funds privately. During the fourth trip to the Solomons in 2000, the team visited the many sites to see what's needed in terms of steps, handrails, and toilet and water facilities. But more importantly, the team met with the nation's prime minister and the premiers of the East, Central, and Western provinces, all of whom pledged their support. [2001 note]

Chapter 34

They Were Truly Loyal!

I was sitting around the School Board Office in St. Martinville, planning the mini-courses I would teach in the fall, the objectives of a state educational grant. The phone rang and Louise was on the other end, telling me that I had received a call from Bill Fisher and that I should get back to him as soon as possible. I dropped everything on my desk and returned home to contact Bill. *Trip number three* to Guadalcanal was on the front burner! Bill and I, representing the Battle of Guadalcanal and Solomon Islands Foundation, would return to meet the local government personnel.

Thanks to Bill and his friend Fred Smith of Federal Express, details of the coming trip would run smoothly. Fred obtained first-class, round-trip tickets to Guadalcanal via Sydney and Brisbane, Australia. He also had personnel from Australia to take care of details along the route. What a friend! Bill had already made progress with Minister of Home Affairs and Deputy Prime Minister Dennis Lulei during our 1995 trip. John Innes, managing director of TechniSyst in Honiara, acted as our liaison and coordinated details with David Vouza. David Vouza, a member of parliament on Guadalcanal, had come to the United States in 1993.

I had on my "track shoes" and quickly called Continental

Airlines to book a flight (#1025), leaving Lafayette at 6:45 AM (0645 hours) on Thursday, July 11, 1996, and arriving in Houston at 7:35 AM (0735 hours). Departing for Los Angeles at 8:25 AM (0825 hours), I arrived there at 9:39 AM (0939 hours). I had begun to outrace the sun. I quickly got my visa for Australia and soon was speaking with Bill Fisher, who had arrived at the QANTAS ticket counter too late to pick up his visa. But now, let Bill take up the narrative.*

I arrived at the QANTAS ticket counter to learn that I needed a visa! A visa for Australia? I couldn't believe it. In all the trips in and out of Europe in the past several years, a passport yes, but a visa? I was really concerned since the flight departed at 1300 (1 p.m.) and it was already 11:30. Fortunately the customer service fellow took over. He took my passport and faxed a copy to Canberra explaining the circumstances. They faxed back temporary permission to enter, but that I had to report to immigration forthwith. . . .

We landed in Sydney after 14 hours of some very excellent weather and too much food. It seemed like we were always being handed food. In reality, we had three great meals and some exceptional snacks.

The flight path into Sydney took us over the city. The night lights were flickering all over as if it were a Christmas tree. The famous Sydney bridge, called the "coat-hanger" by some, really stood out. [My last view of the Coathanger was Christmas of 1942.—J. D.] When we arrived at the terminal there was a customer service rep waiting. She immediately took us to the head of the line and right on through to the immigration where the

---

*The lengthy quotes in this chapter are from *Personnel*, Major Bill Fisher's column in the Covington *Leader*, Covington, Tennessee. With his permission, I have used several of his columns from July and August 1996.

lady agent greeted me with a big smile and a "we'll have this
done in a moment."

We made our connecting flight all right. But while waiting in
the passenger lounge, I asked the customer service rep about a
motel close by the airport in Brisbane. Since we would be spend-
ing several hours there and both Jeff DeBlanc and I were
bushed, it seemed a good idea to get some rest. The rep said not
to worry, someone would tell us about motels when we arrived.
As we entered the terminal lobby from the plane, an agent identified himself as Paul Maltby. Paul had a list of motels along with
a recommendation. He also had us a taxi voucher and a meal
voucher. Thanks to Paul and QANTAS, we spent a restful night
and enjoyed a continental style breakfast. The morning we
spent at the international terminal and in the QANTAS Club.
Now, that was a real treat! We had a panoramic view, good coffee, juice and the latest newspaper.

I was on pins and needles as we approached Brisbane. John
Keenan, the coastwatcher whom I had not seen since 1943, would
meet me at Brisbane International Airport. In the morning, we
were met by John and his lovely wife, Phyllis. We had forty-five
minutes of picture taking, bridging a gap of fifty-three years, and
exchanging gifts. Bill Fisher was kind enough to take pictures and
let me do my thing. We were in tears when we left John and
Phyllis. John looked great but was suffering from cancer. After
farewells, we boarded the plane for Guadalcanal. The trip took
about three hours. Soon, I could make out the shoreline and
Henderson Field. From the cockpit, I captured on video some
really great pictures of the landing and of the "cow pasture."

John Innes greeted us at the airport. On the way to his home
west of Honiara, he briefed us. His home was situated at a spot
on the hillside where we could sit on his upstairs open veranda

and see Tulagi, the Florida Islands, and Savo Island. What a view!

The purpose of our trip was to sit down with local government personnel and work out the possibilities of securing monumental sites for the various scenes of battle around Henderson Field in 1942, including Fighter One and Fighter Two. Bill was a member of Carlson's Raiders and I was a member of the Cactus Air Force. We were there during the battles of October and November 1942 until well into the summer of 1943. Bill would trace the ground sites and I would verify the air approaches to Henderson Field, Fighter One (the cow pasture), and Fighter Two. Of course, we had with us the man who could lead us through the sites, John Innes, originally from Brisbane, Australia. Through the good offices of Jim Wheeler of Federal Express and Peter Framton of QANTAS, Bill and I were able to come here to represent the Battle of Guadalcanal and Solomon Islands Foundation. We would meet with Mr. Wilson Maetau, Director of Tourism in Honiara. We would also meet with the principal planner and assist him and John Innes in selecting battle sites to be reserved and protected by the government. This was a critical step before the main body of government personnel. Bill and I kept busy during the next few days, going to sites to refresh our memories.

I must say at this time that I was fascinated by this tour. I knew that the Japanese had surrounded Henderson Field. However, as an aviator flying off the cow pasture in a fighter plane, I had absolutely no idea how close they really were! I followed the sites in awe and with open mouth when I realized how near we really were to being overrun and killed by Colonel Ichiki's crack troops.

Colonel Ichiki must have figured that the Americans were soft and that they were lousy night fighters. Shortly after midnight, he had his troops perform a *Banzi* attack. They were considered the best of Japanese fighting men. He had his men sever the heads of a Catholic priest and two Catholic nuns on the previous afternoon near Aola, a village on the east side of Henderson Field. He also captured Sergeant Major Jacob Vouza, a retired Guadalcanal police officer who happened to have an American flag hidden in his lavalava. Vouza, refusing to answer questions about the Americans, was tied to a tree, beaten with rifle butts, stabbed in the chest and throat with a sword, shot three times, rendered unconscious, and assumed to be dead. After the enemy left, Vouza revived, chewed through his ropes, and began dragging himself toward the American perimeter, arriving as the fight on the beach was winding down just before sunrise.

Martin Clemens found Vouza and brought him to General Vandegrift's headquarters, where he gave vital information about Ichiki's troops. He was then sent to a hospital where American doctors nursed him to recovery. He was later knighted in London by the Queen of England. When Colonel Ichiki made his third attempt to break through the defenses of the Illu River (three-quarters of a mile from Fighter One, the cow pasture), his men were wiped out by heavy Marine fire on the Illu site and the beach adjacent to it.*

The next site was Edson's Ridge. This ridge overlooked Fighter One from a distance of two miles. This was where

---

*The 1998 movie *Saving Private Ryan*, starring Tom Hanks, triggered in Bill Fisher a flashback to Mount Austen. He even sent me an email reminding me to see this movie. I followed his instructions. I also enjoyed *The Thin Red Line*, starring Nick Nolte and Sean Penn—superbly photographed and directed, but heavy on symbolism! I would later meet the actor Tom Hanks and the director Steven Spielberg on June 6, 2000, at the opening of the D-Day Museum in New Orleans, Louisiana, now the National World War II Museum.

"Pistol Pete," the Japanese mortar expert, would shell us when we created huge dust clouds upon take-off from the cow pasture. I had to sit down and take a few deep breaths of air! This was not from exhaustion. I was now in a position to understand why we were boresighted back in 1942 by this Japanese gun position. Had I known this at the time, I would have set this entire hillside afire with .50-caliber machine guns. Of course, we had no idea of the location. Standing on the site, I could see all of Henderson Field and the cow pasture. Thanks to Lieutenant Colonel Merritt A. Edson (called "Red Mike" because of his red hair) and his troops, the Japanese were stopped cold and we secured the hill.

The next site would take some time to get to, so we rested for the remainder of the day. We had three more sites to visit: Mount Austen and the Gifu and the Matanikau River areas. These were the scenes of the most action. We pushed strongly to have these protected and not sold to homebuilders.

To enhance our point of view, both Bill Fisher and I were guests at a meeting of the South Pacific Tourism Commission held in Honiara. Both of us were asked to speak and we did. We were interviewed by the local radio station and both local newspapers (weeklies). In all cases, we explained the foundation and its purpose. Mr. John Baura, the Permanent Secretary, also spoke.

The then *ad hoc* Battle of Guadalcanal and Solomon Islands Foundation is now recognized by the Government of the Solomon Islands. We expect to have a letter from the Prime Minister in the very near future. From our side, Dick Backus and Bill Fisher are planning another meeting, at which time Nancy Ferrell and Dave Gaddis will report on their visit to Guadalcanal.

The trip to Mount Austen was enlightening for me but a

nostalgic one for Bill. John Innes drove us there in his station wagon. From the top, I could look down the runway of Henderson Field. Now I understand why this spot was necessary to hold. Bill had a friend, a lieutenant in his outfit, who was wounded in the neck during this action and died the next day. Medical aid perhaps could have saved him, but the action was too fierce to obtain this help. To this date, this site continues, in my estimation, to haunt Bill. Every trip I made with him to the Solomons, his friend's name came up. Forensic personnel from Pearl Harbor accompanied us on this trip. Bodies were found near the mouth of the Matanikau River. Since they were here, maybe we could locate the grave of the lieutenant. It has not been located to this date.

The next site was the Gifu. This is the location of the action of Mitch Paige, a machine gunner who for his heroic stand received the Medal of Honor. The last site was the mouth of the Matanikau River. It was here that bones were discovered and, hence, the reason for the team from Pearl. It was thought that the fourteen bodies dug up by the team belonged to the Goettge Patrol. Such was not the case. All of the bodies were Japanese. They were turned over to the Japanese authorities for cremation. Bill and I were glad to have traced these routes and record them on VCR film.

Here are some highlights of the Goettge Patrol. Soon after the Guadalcanal landings on August 7, 1942, Lieutenant Colonel Frank Goettge, an intelligence officer, heard that a white flag had been seen west of the Matanikau River. With General Vandegrift's reluctant consent, he elected to lead a patrol himself to investigate the possibility of a Japanese surrender. Regrettably, they were overwhelmed and cruelly massacred! It must be said that the Japanese did not set a trap. The "white flag" was likely only a regular Japanese battle flag that, by coincidence, was furled, concealing the central red disk. After the massacre, an American detachment was landed west of Point Cruz, made a sweeping maneuver, but made no enemy contact.

My part of the action was a chopper flight over Guadalcanal from Cape Esperance to Aola. I traced the route of the flight patterns we flew when returning from the Slot to the cow pasture, Fighter One. This was also recorded on film. We returned to our host's residence. John Innes had an excellent patio for us to do our homework and record potential sites for possible future monuments comparable to those at Shiloh.

We also had time to look around and check out the flora and fauna of the Solomons. I could associate well with the sounds of birds in the jungle near John Innes's home. I would get up before dawn and listen to the birds. It brought back memories of my brief stay on Kolombangara after I was shot down. When the birds are singing at dawn, all is well. If they are not, then something is amiss!

Today, the whole world is fiberoptically connected. During this trip, I was able to fax letters to my son Jeff Jr. in Henderson, Louisiana, and receive faxes from him. During my other son Richard's trip to Guam, he did the same. This is truly mindboggling! More and more people have CD players, VCRs, personal computers, satellite dishes, and other such marvels of contemporary technology.

There seems to be no limit on the advance of technology— microelectronic technology, globalization of the economy, swift movement of capital, and the shift from an economy based on the manufacture of goods to one based on information and services. Some day, in the far future, man will learn to store knowledge in the structure of space itself and be able to preserve his thoughts in frozen waves of light for as long as the universe lasts!

[We] had the opportunity between business meetings and site visits to assume a tourist posture. There is plenty to see and do in and around the Solomon Islands.

Take the birds for instance. The Islands have members of the parrot family galore. There are Lorikeets, colorful green, red, blue and with some golden yellow mixed in. Then come the Cockatoos. The pair I saw flying and cackling about the home of our host, John Innes, are white as the new snow. They tended to dominate all of the other birds. Of course, there is the Solomon's most famous bird, the Eclectus, a most gorgeous fowl. Bright blues, reds and greens adorn this most sociable parrot.

The above birds are in abundance and are sold regularly by the natives for about SI $30, which is roughly US $10. The government is quite willing, under certain circumstances and with prior permission, to allow the birds out of the country. Unfortunately our government decided to ban all imports as of October of 1994. The stated reason is to protect the birds. That, however, would seem to fall within the purview of the local authorities, not Uncle Sam. The most likely real reason is to protect American breeders. An Eclectus sells for about $2000.

Fishing in and around Guadalcanal is pretty good. Brice [W. Schuller], another guest of John's, is in the fishing business. The natives bring Brice a type of lobster which he in turn ships live to Hong Kong at a tidy profit. One night he brought home several two-inch slices of King Fish. We fried two of them up and away they went! . . .

Back in the bush lurk other varmints. The inhabitants are lizards three feet long and nine foot crocodiles in the rivers at some spots. One can meet centipedes 20 inches long and poisonous. The Megapod bird sometimes will lay eggs way up the Lunga River. They bury the eggs where it is warm and it is up to the chicks to get out and make it. Their main breeding and laying spot is on Savo Island. Savo is in fact a dormant volcano so that the soil is warm and does the incubating. The Islanders will hunt for the eggs, as they are considered a delicacy.

Life can be easy. A taxi might cost a bit of a dollar for the short trips and the longer ones are negotiable. One of the newer hotels is the Iron Bottom Sound Hotel. It is a little west of the center of town, but one can enjoy quite a bit of privacy facing the Sea Lark Channel. The rooms are small by our standards, but modern in every respect, including the bath facilities. The food tends towards Chinese and Philippine and is well prepared and reasonably priced.

Native crafts abound and the price is always a matter of two people arriving at an agreement. Never pay the asking price. And also don't buy or pick up war souvenirs or gold. Both will be offered to you on the street and both are illegal and will be confiscated upon departure. Under special circumstances, one can get a letter from the Minister of Tourism to carry off a small non-dangerous war item.

The best way to get there is to connect up with QANTAS in Los Angeles. From there one can change in Sydney, Australia or Nandi, Fiji Islands. Both will require an overnight stay. The connecting Solomon Air only makes two trips a week to Nandi and to Brisbane. Relax and have fun.

PS: If you have ever wondered why QANTAS is spelled without a "U," the letters stand for Queensland And Northern Territories Air Service.

Now the *bombshell*. When we returned to the States, I received an email from Bill Fisher that brought me upright in my chair. Bill said that he received a call from John Innes, who asked him to pass along a message to me. Mr. Milner Tozaka, a former Permanent Secretary to the Solomon Islands government, recently made a trip up to the area where I had been shot down during the war, Kolombangara and Vella La Vella. While there, he met an old man who said that he was one of the two natives who had paddled Jim Feliton and me to the Navy plane that came to rescue us. John was satisfied that this was true but suggested that I call Mr. Tozaka himself. Tozaka apparently had items from the islander in question, reflecting this moment in time. Well, I am not naive enough to believe all this without verification, although I do trust John's judgment. I decided to test this information via mail contact with Tozaka.

In the meantime, as fate would have it, I received a letter from John Keenan's wife, Phyllis, giving me new information about John and his cancer condition. The latter part of the letter struck me between the eyes. Her granddaughter was doing research on the coastwatchers for a high-school social studies course. She happened to run across a diary in the attic of the Keenan home, tucked away since the war. For military reasons, coastwatchers were not supposed to keep diaries. But John kept one, turning it over to the proper authorities after our rescue from Vella La Vella and his subsequent reassignment, after February 1943, to Bougainville Island. After the war, the diary was returned to John, who stored it and, over the years, apparently forgot about it until it was discovered by his granddaughter.

John had a copy of Walter Lord's book, *Lonely Vigil: Coastwatchers of the Solomons*. My picture complete with Japanese uniform and the native spear and my account of the rescue and dates matched the dates in his log!* The best part is that the diary reflected the name of the islander who rescued me from

*See chapter 20.

Kolombangara and subsequently brought me to Keenan. Armed with this information, I wrote to Mr. Tozaka and obtained the name of the man whom he claimed was the one in question.

After a few letters exchanged over a period of months, I was informed that the man's name is Atitao Lodukolo and that he is now more than eighty years old. I was also informed that Mr. Tozaka's mother was the young girl and daughter of the village chief who gave us that wonderful fish meal before we were rescued. I quickly checked with John Keenan for verification. John had already identified in his diary the man's name as Ati. In a letter of February 18, 1997, I asked John if I could send a copy of this portion of his diary to Milner Tozaka for verification. The diary confirmed the story. Keenan knew him as Ati, his trusted scout. I received a photo of Mr. Atitao. We are in correspondence via Mr. Tozaka.

Ati's health is good. He is starting a project for his family. He asked if I could help out with a few items. I sent him US $700. I shall take up his case with the foundation and see if we can help out a man who not only saved my skin, but also that of other pilots and men of the cruiser *Helena* sunk off the coast of Vella La Vella.* It is my wish that this could be an additional goal of the foundation.

I hoped to meet Ati again. I had run full circle with both Henry Josselyn, whom I met again in Ipswich, England, in 1975 during my sojourn in the Netherlands, and John Keenan, in 1996 during a stopover in Brisbane, Australia. These coastwatchers are now both deceased. John Keenan died on April 11, 1997, at the age of eighty-one. I hoped that I may go full

---

*See Walter Lord's *Lonely Vigil: Coastwatchers of the Solomons* for details of the *Helena*'s sinking.

circle with the Solomon islanders who aided me and others back in World War II. With God's help, I hoped to be able to fulfill my obligations to these fine islanders. We were fortunate to have such helpers. We were losing the war in the Solomons in 1942 and the natives generally stuck with a winner. Those who helped the coastwatchers could see through the Japanese deception. They were truly loyal!

Epilogue

The Dawning of the
Twenty-first Century

The long-awaited meeting with Ati took place on Sunday, May 7, 2000, on Vella La Vella, during my fourth trip to the Solomons.* As our plane approached Vella La Vella and over-flew Bilua, I zeroed in on the route where fifty-seven years ago, I approached this very island with Ati and others in a twelve-man canoe. From the plane, I noticed that the red barn and the church were gone! I saw an old home at the site that had the appearance of Reverend Silvester's domicile, where I had spent the night so many years ago.

From the air, we shot video of the site and we proceeded on to a logging airstrip in the mountains a few miles up the north coast of Vella. I started to correct the pilot and to remind him that we were not heading toward the spot where I was brought to Henry Josselyn and John Keenan's hideout 3,000 feet in the mountains. The outpost was located above Mundi Mundi on the southwest portion of Vella La Vella and above Chief Silas's home at Paramata. The Japanese outpost located near Iringila

*Trip number four was a two-week expedition to the Solomons in the spring of 2000. The agenda for the team included the survey over six sites and a flight to the Western Solomons (Ghizo, Vella La Vella, and Kennedy Islands). Without going into too much detail, this team of five would gather data and design each battle site comparable to those in the United States— Civil War sites, for instance. This would attract more American tourists and enhance the economy of the islands.

(northwestern part of Vella) was clearly visible from the 3,000-foot-high coastwatchers' station. The pilot told me that the airstrip we were going to was the site where we were to meet Ati. I captured the landing approach and touch-down on video.

Once on the ground, we switched over to *powered* canoes (times have changed!). It took us only thirty-five minutes to reach Ati's home. The boat arrived at a wharf adjacent to the native village. I was in the lead canoe and nearly capsized the whole works in my eagerness to get out. The dock was beautifully decorated with flowers and enhanced with a sign welcoming our group.

I spotted an aged islander, holding a staff, with a hibiscus over his left ear. Ati is well into his nineties. He reminded me of Moses. Standing beside him was a young man who had the appearance of Ati as I remembered him so many years ago. Was this his grandson? I came ashore and we shook hands and hugged. I even threw my hat high into the air, yelling, "Full circle!" As we mingled with Ati and his relatives, they presented us with leis. Smiling, the members of his family let our group know that we were most welcome in their village. Ati and I were repeatedly photographed shaking hands.

Ati and I exchanged gifts. He gave me *bakiha,* traditional island currency that is made with fossilized clamshell fashioned into donut-shaped pieces. This *bakiha* symbolizes the eternal bonding of the Lodukolo and DeBlanc families. I gave him five US $20 bills.

Soon we were escorted to a native home for refreshments. It was then that I noticed that Ati had to be helped. He still had that "proud look" and self-confidence that I remembered. However, his gait was slow as I held his arm and escorted him to the hut. He wore no sandals. Although we had to walk over sharp coral rocks, his face showed no change of expression.

Once inside, Ati and I were seated side by side in our respective chairs. A third chair was brought in and another islander entered and sat down. She turned out to be Mrs. Dalcy Tozaka, daughter of Chief Silas of Vella La Vella and mother of George Milner Tozaka. She was the young girl fifty-seven years ago who fed Feliton and me that tasty meal. She graciously stood up and presented me with a gift for Louise. It is a beautiful handmade bag in basket-weave. It was a pleasant surprise. I accepted the gift and said, as I handed her a ten-dollar bill, "Louise wanted me to look up the young girl who had fed us and give her a tip." In this way I supplied the belated courtesy I could not have done years before.

The food was delicious, as always. I spoke with Ati via an interpreter since he still speaks mostly pidgin English. It was then that he mentioned the Japanese uniform I wore, the spear, etc., which cemented our encounter so many years ago. When he mentioned that five of his men left after I put on the Japanese uniform, I asked why. Ati said that they thought I was Japanese. I quickly stated that, with my green eyes, I could not possibly have been mistaken for a Japanese. He simply smiled at that remark. We talked far into the afternoon about our journey through the bush of Kolombangara, Ghizo, and Vella La Vella. We also spoke about the rescue of the survivors of the U.S.S. *Helena.*

He also mentioned that he is building a "Coastwatchers' Haven" for tourists near his present village. This was his reason for requesting my help in his business venture for his family. I had given him some money to help him, a mere token for the priceless bag of rice with which he ransomed me.*

---

*Over the years, one U.S. newspaper article had me captured by the Japanese, who then sold me for a bag of rice! Another had me "captured by head-hunting cannibals, where he was given a sack of rice to eat in a small cage"!

Of course, fifty-seven years had passed since Ati saved my life. Ati had saved many others after my rescue and even played a very significant role in the 1943 rescue of the men from the sunken U.S.S. *Helena.* Henry Josselyn had the foresight to group the survivors as they were picked off the beach. Henry knew that the Japanese were searching for survivors and were very active along the northern coast of Vella. He even had his scouts keeping an eye open for all enemy activities at Lambu Lambu, Java, and Paraso, three of the Japanese outposts besides the one he was covering at Iringila.

Henry had the help of Missionary Silvester and Corporal Ati. Each was given a portion of the 165 men rescued from the *Helena.* Josselyn took his group into the bush near Paraso. Rev. Silvester went bush with his survivors at Java, and Ati rounded up the many "strays" drifting individually ashore between Maravari and Lambu Lambu and went bush between Maravari and Barakoma.

Here was the answer to my thoughts! Of course, Ati's village was located near the site where his group of survivors went bush so many years ago. This was the reason for building his "Coastwatchers' Haven" at this location, the one I helped him with financially.

It was time for us to part since the weather was closing in and we had to return over 250 miles back to Henderson Field. Amid the waving and cheering of the islanders in Ati's village, our plane took off for the return to Guadalcanal, stopping off on Ghizo.

On the return trip we again flew over the Reverend Silvester's mission. I wanted to see if a trip to this spot would produce pictures for this last chapter. Weather conditions were not too favorable and daylight was running out.

We landed at Ghizo to pick up Major Bill Fisher, who had

remained there while I went to Vella La Vella to see Ati. Fisher's mission was to tie the JFK and other sites in the Western Solomons into the foundation project. This caused our schedule to be extended another hour as we were taken to Kennedy Island (formerly Plum Pudding Island) to consider what has to be done to ensure tourists participation here.

Semper Fidelis, you guys and gals. Let us keep alive the "dream" for the Solomon sites and Ati's project.